AESTHETICS AND FILM

Continuum Aesthetics

Series Editor: Derek Matravers, Open University and University of Cambridge, UK

The Continuum Aesthetics Series looks at the aesthetic questions and issues raised by all major art forms. Stimulating, engaging and accessible, the series offers food for thought not only for students of aesthetics, but also for anyone with an interest in philosophy and the arts.

Titles available from Continuum:
Aesthetics and Architecture, Edward Winters
Aesthetics and Literature, David Davies
Aesthetics and Morality, Elisabeth Schellekens
Aesthetics and Music, Andy Hamilton

Forthcoming in 2008
Aesthetics and Painting, Jason Gaiger
Aesthetics and Nature, Glenn Parsons

AESTHETICS AND FILM

KATHERINE THOMSON-JONES

continuum

Continuum International Publishing Group

The Tower Building
11 York Road
London
SE1 7NX

80 Maiden Lane
Suite 704
New York
NY 10038

www.continuumbooks.com

British Library Cataloguing-in-Publication Data
A catalogue record for this book is available from the British Library.

ISBN 10: HB: 0-8264-8522-7

PB: 0-8264-8523-5

ISBN 13: HB: 978-0-8264-8522-9

PB: 978-0-8264-8523-6

Library of Congress Cataloging-in-Publication Data
A catalog record for this book is available from the Library of Congress.

Typeset by Newgen Imaging Systems Pvt Ltd, Chennai, India
Printed and bound in Great Britain by MPG Books Ltd, Bodmin, Cornwall

CONTENTS

CONTENTS

PREFACE

Among philosophies of the arts, philosophy of film is distinguished by the extent to which it draws upon the broader theoretical tradition for the art form in question. One explanation of the attention philosophers give to film theory has to do with the fact that the technical development and public distribution of film at the end of the nineteenth century did not coincide with wide recognition of its artistic potential. Film had to earn art status in the face of considerable technophobic scepticism. This meant that early film-making practice tended to involve the self-conscious application or demonstration of a theory of art, and early film critical practice involved the explicit articulation and defense of the theories behind the films. In turn this meant that, from the very beginning, film writing was highly philosophical. And although the art status of film has long been secure and the preoccupations of film theorists have broadened considerably, there is still a philosophical self-consciousness to the tradition of film studies.

Broadly speaking, there are three kinds, or developmental phases, of film theory that deal with issues taken up by contemporary philosophers. Classical film theory from the 1920s to the 1950s primarily aimed to defend the emergence of a new art form. Contemporary philosophers who appreciate such classical figures as Rudolph Arnheim, André Bazin and Sergei Eisenstein work to complete or extend aspects of this defence of film art–for example, by considering whether film can represent rather than merely record reality, whether film-making has unique resources for formal play or expression, and whether film is inherently more realistic than other art forms.

The kind of film theory that was dominant in the late 1960s and throughout the 1970s – now commonly referred to just as 'seventies' film theory, involved the application of semiotics, structuralism and psycho-analytic theory to film. Some topics that interest philosophers bridge the periods of classical and seventies, or psycho-semiotic, theory – for example, the topic of authorship, which in the period of classical theory was of interest for its connection to art status, and in the period of psycho-semiotic theory was of interest for its connection to theories of interpretation. The tendency to refer to film in linguistic terms was most powerful during the period of psycho-semiotic film theory. Philosophers are interested to see whether the analogy between film and language can stand up to rigorous analysis and whether drawing such an analogy is helpful for explaining how we understand or interpret films.

Cognitive film theory from the 1980s to the present deals with the nature of our engagement with film. There is a great deal of collaboration and conversation between cognitive film theorists and philosophers. This reflects a shared interest in the application of philosophical, psychological and neurological theories of mind to our understanding of film engagement – how the viewer makes sense of what she sees on screen (and hears on the soundtrack) – particularly in terms of following a story; how she assigns an overall meaning and value to a film; how she supplements what she sees and hears with imagination; and how she responds with feeling to depicted characters and events, as well as to aspects of the look and feel of the film itself.

This book is organized around the issues that interest philosophers who are thinking about the history as well as the contemporary state of both film and film theory. Since these issues are raised by films themselves but have often already been explored by film theorists, the aim here is to make philosophical sense of the theory and, in the process, illuminate something about the nature of film. This is not to say that every question or issue addressed in the book comes to philosophy from film theory. The question of whether narrative fiction films must have narrators, for example, while inspired by work in literary theory, is almost exclusively pursued by philosophers. Nevertheless, the close working relationship between film theory and philosophy is evident throughout the book.

It is important to realize that this is not a book about film *as* philosophy–it will not use films to illustrate or test philosophical views, nor will it present an argument for the equivalence of philosophical systems and film worlds. This is a book which takes film *per se* as the subject of philosophical inquiry. It is thus for anyone who wishes to better understand an art form that continues to adapt to different moving-image media only to increase in its power and appeal.

Given its broad focus on film as an art form, the book will not offer lengthy individual film analyses. As general philosophical claims about film are advanced, however, they will often be brought home to the reader with particular examples. These examples are drawn primarily from narrative fiction film which reflects the focus of the kind of film theory under consideration. This focus is not meant to imply a lack of important theoretical work on or philosophical significance in other kinds of film – say, experimental film or documentary. If anything, this focus simply indicates a starting point for the philosophy of film. Insofar as the forms and genres, as well as the technological resources, of film continue to evolve and expand, there is plenty of exciting philosophical work still to be done. Ultimately, *Aesthetics and Film* aims to offer support and create enthusiasm for this important future work.

I would like to thank the series editor, Derek Matravers, as well as Berys Gaut, Gregory Currie, Andrew Kania, Paisley Livingston, Tess Takahashi, Thomas Wartenberg, George Wilson and Michael Zryd for their invaluable feedback on parts of this book. I would also like to thank Martin Thomson-Jones for his constant support at every stage of the book's preparation.

Katherine Thomson-Jones

CHAPTER 1

FILM AS AN ART

Is film an art? Before we can answer this question, we need to be clear on what we mean by 'film'. The term 'film' is ambiguous; it refers both to an art form that employs a variety of physical media – celluloid, video and digital formats, for example – and also to the traditional medium of the art form – the projected film strip that results from the complex technical processes of filming and editing. Sometimes 'film' is also used to refer to the art form specifically when it employs the traditional film medium. Classical film theorists use the term in this way simply because at the time they were writing, the film medium was the only medium of the art form. Despite this ambiguity, however, there is good reason to hold onto the term 'film'. Most importantly, the term is still widely used by ordinary film-goers, film critics and film theorists, and it covers instances of the art form in every filmmaking tradition, viewed in any setting. Thus in this book, we will keep the term 'film' but use it carefully by marking a three-way distinction between film the art form, film the medium, and 'photographically-based' film – the art form in its traditional medium. We will also follow common usage in keeping the term 'cinematic' to describe a film, an aspect of a film or a mode of engagement with a film that is defined by or relies upon distinctive or unique features of film media.

So how should we understand our original question? – Is film an art? If we are referring to an established art form, then our question is trivial at best. In fact, however, the first answer to this question established the possibility of using the term 'film' to refer to a medium-specific art form. In the early days of film, first-generation classical film theorists were interested in the artistic possibilities inherent in traditional filmmaking processes, particularly in cinematography. Insofar as cinematography produces a recording on a celluloid strip to be run through a projector, classical film theorists were thinking about the artistic possibilities of the film medium. But not surprisingly, the way they established that film can be art is by scrutinizing the results of using the medium – the films projected onto a screen for an audience. It was because early film theorists glimpsed artistry on the screen that they decided that the product of cinematography, editing and celluloid projection could be art. Nowadays, of course, 'film' still refers to an art form but not to a medium-specific one. As we shall see, this raises the question of how to uphold the status of an art form which was originally justified in terms of a particular medium when that art form has moved beyond its traditional medium. Before we consider this question, however, let's examine the original justification – how film first became art.

To answer our starting question, we might begin by pointing out the existence of cinematic masterpieces like *New World* (2006) or *The Seven Samurai* (1954). But does this show that (photographically-based) film *per se* is an art? It all depends on what makes such films masterpieces – whether it is their inherently cinematic qualities or whether it is qualities derived from other, established art forms – for example, their dramatic qualities or their painterly qualities of composition. The real question, then, is whether film is an art form in its own right and the answer to this question will depend on whether what makes a film a film can also be what makes it art.

Today most film-goers assume without question that film media can serve artistic purposes. When film first emerged, however, as a mechanical innovation in recording, there was no such assumption. If anything, in fact, there was an opposing assumption that film is merely a recording device devoid of artistic interest. This meant that early filmmakers and film theorists first had to legitimate their practices before they could secure a receptive audience. Rudolph Arnheim, one of the most prominent early film theorists, was well aware of how much he had to prove for the sake of an emerging art form. Both the 1933 and the 1957 versions of his treatise on the art of silent film provide a detailed catalogue of all the creative and expressive possibilities inherent in the filmmaking process. Essentially, Arnheim accepts the assumption that mere mechanical recording cannot be art and then argues that film art begins where mechanical recording ends. The result is an authoritative articulation of the anti-realist principles of silent filmmaking.[1]

We see these principles applied in different ways in each of the major silent film movements. In Soviet montage films like Sergei Eisenstein's *Battleship Potemkin* (1925), editing is used to break up, rearrange and change the meaning of the recording. In German expressionist films like *The Cabinet of Dr. Caligari* (1920), highly stylized sets, acting and narration are emphasized with incongruous camerawork and lighting.

Even the films of Charlie Chaplin with their use of visual tricks embody principles for establishing a break with reality and the creation of something entirely new.

But what of the assumption that film cannot be art if it is mere mechanical recording? Behind this assumption is the following line of thought: When a film is made, however much thought and creativity go into writing the script, constructing a scene and rehearsing the actors, once the camera is rolling, that's it: the next crucial stage is beyond the creative control of the filmmakers. Of course the cinematographer can creatively control the angle, direction and distance of the camera, and the editor can creatively control the order and rhythm of images in the final cut. But no one can creatively control the content of those images – if the camera mechanically records a tree, then you end up with an image of just that tree, just as it looked at the moment of recording. It is this lack of artistic control at the crucial and distinctively photographic moment of the filmmaking process that allegedly prevents photographically-based film from being an art form.

It is undoubtedly true that film is separated from traditional arts like painting and drama by the mechanical nature of its recording process. The further question is whether mechanical recording rules out artistry. Actually, there are really two questions here: the question of whether there can be artistry *despite* mechanical recording and the question of whether there can be artistry *in* mechanical recording itself. Early film theorists like Arnheim only considered the first of these two questions. The second question is taken up by the first generation of sound film theorists. Among them is the great André Bazin who we meet in the next chapter on realism, and who locates the power of film in the immediacy and accessibility of its recorded imagery.

By the time we get to the second chapter we shall be able to appreciate that Bazin's work is made possible by the prior work of silent film theorists in legitimizing filmmaking and film study. In particular, Arnheim's work is historically important for establishing a certain theoretical approach to film, one involving close analysis of everything that makes film a unique artistic medium. Since we are interested, not just in confirming the art status of photographically-based film, but confirming its independent art status, this kind of medium-specific analysis is extremely useful. It is not, however, the only valid theoretical approach to film given that there are many continuities between film and other art forms. We will become particularly aware of these continuities when we discuss authorship and narration in Chapters 3 and 5, respectively.

Without medium-specific analysis, however, we might be stuck at the view that individual films can be art when they successfully record art but film *per se* cannot be art. On this view, film is not an independent art form because the filming process does not contribute to the artistic value of the final product. This brings our attention to the fact that film theorists who want to defend the art status of film are up against two distinct arguments, both of which involve the assumption that film cannot be art if it is mere mechanical recording. On the first view, film is treated as the mechanical recording of real life; on the second view, film is treated as the mechanical recording of the established art of drama and is thus 'canned theatre'. While Arnheim responds to the first view, contemporary philosophers of film have tended to focus on the second view. This is partly because the canned-theatre argument has been revisited by the contemporary philosopher, Roger Scruton.

In his much-discussed essay, 'Photography and Representation', Scruton argues that films are just photographs of more or less artistically valuable dramatic representations.[2] Films cannot be artistic representations themselves because photographs are not the kind of thing that can represent: Their mechanical production blocks any artistic interpretation of what is being photographed. The debate concerning the art status of film is thus not merely of historical interest. Scruton's contemporary challenge reminds us that a proper understanding of film requires an examination of the grounds for assuming, as most of us do, that film is an art. In other words, Scruton reminds us that as philosophers we are committed to uncovering and testing the most basic beliefs that inform our practices as filmviewers, filmcritics and filmmakers.

SCRUTON: AGAINST FILM AS AN ART

Scruton's refutation of film as an art form has three steps: First, he assumes that the film medium is an inherently photographic medium. Then he creates an argument against the possibility of photographs being representational art. And finally, he extends this argument to film.

In order to assess Scruton's argument against film art, therefore, we need to assess his argument against photographic art; that is, unless we discover that Scruton's argument against photographic art cannot legitimately be extended to film. A photograph that has not been manipulated in any way records the appearance of its subject. But, Scruton insists, this does not mean that the photograph represents its subject. A painting of the very same subject, on the other hand, does represent its subject. What's the difference?

To answer this question, we need to understand how Scruton's account of representation focuses on the relation, established in its production, between an image and its subject. This relation determines the kind of interest we can take in the image – whether aesthetic or merely instrumental. To take an aesthetic interest in a representational work of art is to take an interest in *how* the work represents its subject. Scruton claims that photographs fail to inspire this kind of interest; instead they only inspire interest in *what* is represented, namely the subject itself. The photograph is therefore dispensable as a means to satisfy our curiosity about the subject. What makes the difference here is the way an image is produced – whether through mechanical recording or through the intentional, interpretive activity of a representational artist.

According to Scruton, a painting like the *Mona Lisa* is representational because it shows us how the artist saw the subject. The style of the painting manifests da Vinci's decisions about how to paint his subject and makes the painting interesting whether or not the subject is also interesting. Moreover, given that the painting is the product of artistic intentions, the subject need not even have existed. Compare this to an imaginary case of a photograph showing a woman dressed and made-up to look like the subject of the *Mona Lisa*. Clearly this is neither a photograph of a Renaissance gentlewoman nor a photograph of a non-existent woman in the mind's eye of the photographer. The photograph cannot be either because the subject has to exist and be in front of the camera to be photographed. It is not up to the photographer to create the subject and, as a result, it is not up to the photographer to decide how the subject is going to look in the photograph. Since the camera simply records how an actual subject actually looked at a certain moment in time, the resulting image has no aesthetic interest as an artist's interpretation.

When we look at a painting, knowing that it is the product of intentional activity, we assume that its perceptible details were chosen as part of the style of the work and thus have meaning. In contrast, when we look at a photograph, we assume that its details were not chosen. In fact, if it is a true photograph, those details could not have been chosen: they are just the result of the camera automatically recording all the details of the subject itself. Scruton insists that it is precisely this alleged lack of control over detail on the part of the photographer that prevents her product from being representational art. Moreover, it is the same lack of control in recording that prevents films from being representational art. This is the point at which Scruton extends his argument from photography to film:

> A film is a photograph of a dramatic representation; it is not, because it cannot be, a photographic representation. It follows that if there is such a thing as a cinematic masterpiece it will be so because – like *Wild Strawberries* and *Le règle du jeu* – it is in the first place a dramatic masterpiece.[3]

Scruton goes further to suggest that it is not just that the film-recording process is neutral in terms of its contribution to the dramatic success of the final work, but that it actually makes a negative contribution: Again due to a lack of control over the detail in film images, it is going to be harder for a film audience to know how to interpret a recorded dramatic scene than for a theatre audience to know how to interpret an analogous scene on stage. Let's say that we have a film scene and a stage scene of a battle. Since the camera records everything in the scene – every splatter of mud, every glint of steel – the film audience can be overwhelmed with and distracted by a plethora of unorganized detail. In contrast, since the staging of a battle in a play is stylized to allow for the foregrounding of certain features of the landscape and certain actions, the theatre audience is properly drawn to the dramatic locus of the scene.

RESPONDING TO SCRUTON

According to Scruton, since a photograph records rather than represents its subject, it cannot support an aesthetic interest in how its subject is shown. All it can support is an interest in the subject itself. A film is just a series of photographs and thus also fails to represent. We cannot take an aesthetic interest in how something is shown on film because how that thing is shown is merely the result of a mechanical recording process and not the result of creative artistic choices.

Given this line of argument, there are at least two strategies for responding to Scruton's claim against film:

1. Accept that Scruton's argument against photography automatically extends to film and then show that there are some photographs in which we can take an aesthetic interest and which thereby qualify as art in their own right.

2. Leave unquestioned Scruton's argument against photography and instead question its extension to film.

The defence of photographic art involved in the first strategy is convincingly made by William King in the appropriately titled, 'Scruton and Reasons for Looking at Photographs'.[4] The second strategy involves pointing to ways in which film is unlike photography, ways that suggest the requisite creative control for representation. The most significant way in which film is unlike photography is of course in being a sequence of images that are combined in any way that the film artist wants through editing.[5] There are, however, a whole range of devices and conventions that are distinctive to film and that can serve artistic purposes. These are helpfully catalogued for us by Arnheim.

Before we turn back to Arnheim, however, let's consider King's response to Scruton. Remember that Scruton takes it as evidence of the inability of photographs to represent that the only reason we can have for looking at them is to satisfy our curiosity about their subjects. This way of thinking about photographs, King responds, can only be a result of a lack of awareness or appreciation of the range of photographic techniques and the consequent range of possibilities for artistic intervention in the photographic process. If Scruton had actually considered real examples of photographs and the way people talk about them, he would have realized that there are many kinds of reason for looking at a photograph. As well as curiosity about the subject, there are reasons having to do with the evocative power of the image, its formal properties, and its history of production. Most importantly, however, reasons for looking at non-abstract 'art photography' invariably include an interest in the manner of representation.

King gives us three compelling examples of photographs which involve artistic interpretation: William Klein's 'Entrance to Beach, Ostia, Italy, 1956', Ansel Adams's 'Moon and Half Dome', and Ralph Gibson's 'The Priest'. In each case, the photographer has effected an aesthetic transformation of his subject such that the photograph has qualities that the subject does not have. Moreover, this is done solely by photographic means, including the use of different lenses and development methods. Thus Klein distances and renders enigmatic an otherwise slightly threatening group of young men by imposing a grainy 'photographic' texture on the image. Adams lends a quality of unreality to a moon-lit landscape by making objects appear larger and closer than normal. And Gibson formalizes a human subject by framing only the very bottom of the priest's face and the top of his vestments in smooth, sharp contrast.[6]

With these examples, King implies that due to the complexity of the photographic method, the photographer has just as many options for presenting her subject as the painter. If photography can be art and film is essentially photographic, then surely film can be art too. This is not enough to show that film is its own art form, however. We need a sense of the differences between the artistic resources of photography and film, something that Arnheim indirectly supplies. But Arnheim only takes us so far in accounting for the artistic claims of film. It is up to contemporary scholars to complete the account by suggesting that film offers more creative possibilities than almost any other art form, including painting and drama.

ARNHEIM: THE *LIMITATIONS* OF FILM MAKE IT AN ART

Arnheim's argument for photographically-based film as an art form has two stages. First he catalogues all the medium-specific ways in which the film image is different from perceived reality. Then he illustrates all the ways in which these peculiarities of the film medium can be exploited for artistic effect. Since Arnheim is working under the assumption that art ought to be expressive, he urges filmmakers to use all aspects of the film medium – from camera angles to editing – as expressively as possible. As a result, what we end up with is a handbook of film techniques for expression and the creation of meaning.

Arnheim is certainly not alone in thinking that film is an expressive medium. What is distinctive about his view, besides its technical detail, is the key assumption about the source of expression in film. According to Arnheim, expression is possible when a film fails to record something accurately. It is precisely in the limitations of film as a mechanical recording device that possibilities for artistic interpretation emerge. It might seem strange to want to affirm the art status of film in such a negative way, and indeed, as we shall see, there are limits to Arnheim's approach. In focusing on the ways in which we fail to experience a film as real life, Arnheim misses all the ways in which we experience a film as more than real life. We'll come to this idea later, however. First let's see how Arnheim responds to the claim that film cannot be art because it is mere mechanical recording.

According to Arnheim, we see that film fails to record accurately in all the discrepancies between perceived reality and the film image.

These include: (1) a discrepancy in perceived depth; (2) a discrepancy in the perceived size and shape of objects; (3) a discrepancy in the limits on our range of view; and, (4) a discrepancy in the experience of the flow of space and time.

The first discrepancy in perceived depth is the result of recording and then projecting three-dimensional, real-life events (or performances) onto the flat surfaces of film stock and screen. With the subsequent loss of depth, the film image is experienced as something in between two and three dimensions. Take the example of an aerial shot of two passing trains. In the three-dimensional world represented on screen, the viewer sees one train moving away from her and one towards her. But on the flat screen she can also see the trains as moving towards the upper and lower edges of the frame.[7] Moreover, this second impression modifies the first so that even in three dimensions there is a significant loss of perceived depth. This is one way, according to Arnheim, in which 'film is most satisfactorily denuded of its realism'.[8]

With the loss of depth comes the loss of what Arnheim calls 'constancies of size and shape' in our perceptual experience. In real life we perceive an object moving away or towards us as remaining constant in size even though the image of the object on our retina changes in size. When we watch a film, on the other hand, an object moving towards the camera appears to grow larger and one moving away from the camera appears to grow smaller. Similarly with shape: in real life we perceive a rectangular table as rectangular even though the image on our retina is wider at the front than at the back. In a film, however, a rectangular table, particularly one close to the camera, may appear wider at the front than at the back.[9] Of course Arnheim is not saying that you are unable to see the rectangular table as rectangular on screen, just that this way of seeing is not automatic.

While the limits of the flat screen contribute to a loss of perceived depth in film, they also contribute to the loss of the full range of vision that we have in everyday life. By moving our eyes and turning our heads, we can see a continuous panorama of our surroundings. But when we watch a film we cannot turn our heads to see beyond the frame. In this way, Arnheim thinks we are reminded once again of the limitations of the filmrecording medium.[10]

Perhaps the most profound discrepancy, however, between perceived reality and the film image is a function of editing. In real life, we cannot jump instantly to 5 minutes later or to 5 miles away. We have to pass through all 5 minutes and cross all 5 miles. Not so in film. A scene at one time and place may be immediately followed by a scene at a totally different time and place. Arnheim suggests that it is the pictorial quality of film that prevents the juxtaposition of scenes and shots from disturbing or confusing the viewer: 'One looks at [the juxtaposed scenes and shots] as calmly as one would at a collection of picture postcards'.[11]

Once Arnheim has listed these and other discrepancies between perceived reality and the film image, he moves onto the second stage of his argument. At this stage, he uses a wide variety of examples to show how the film artist can exploit the failings of film as a mechanical recording device. Behind this project is a particular theory of art, one that can be questioned independently of Arnheim's film analysis. Ultimately, whether Arnheim can succeed in defending the art status of film is going to depend less on his brilliant catalogue of expressive film techniques and more on the acceptability of his criteria for art status.

According to Arnheim, art ought to be expressive in order to serve a definite purpose: By highlighting and consequently drawing our attention to those qualities of things that we would miss in a mechanical recording, expressive art helps us to understand the true nature of things and what they have in common. Now we can begin to see why Arnheim spends so much time listing the failings of film as a recording device. If film were entirely successful in recording exactly how things look, then, as Scruton suggested, film would just give us what everyday experience gives us; namely, an undifferentiated, pragmatic, quantitative view of the world. It is only when film fails to record accurately that expressive patterns can emerge. The world is interpreted for us on film and given meaning.[12] Thus Arnheim urges the film artist not to accept 'shapeless reproduction', but to 'stress the peculiarities of his medium' in a way that 'the objects represented should not thereby be destroyed but rather strengthened, concentrated, interpreted'.[13]

For each of the discrepancies between the film image and perceived reality, Arnheim provides various examples of their expressive potential. Take the loss of depth in the film image and the resulting loss of constancy in the perceived size and shape of objects on screen: Arnheim suggests low-angle shots gain their expressive power as a result of these discrepancies. A close-up, low-angle shot of a police officer communicates forcefulness because the police officer appears to tower above us with a huge body and a small head.[14] This distortion that makes the shot expressive is due entirely to the flattening out of the image and our literal interpretation of its distorted proportions. Moreover, the same conditions of distortion can be used to suggest the relative importance of characters on screen. If one character is significantly closer to the camera than another, the first character appears to dwarf the second, both physically and psychically.[15]

The viewer's loss of an unlimited view due to the framing of the shot has many expressive functions, one of which is the creation of suspense. For example, it is a convention in horror films to show a monster's next victim on screen and leave, at least temporarily, the monster off screen. The frame prevents the viewer from doing what he would normally do; namely, turning his head to get a look at what is making the victim scream. Instead the viewer must imagine the horrors faced by the victim while anxiously awaiting the revelation of the monster.[16]

The final discrepancy mentioned above concerning the continuity of space and time is perhaps the one richest in expressive potential. As we have seen, Arnheim points to the way editing, as an essential component of the film medium, subverts mechanical recording by changing the way we perceive the passage of time and the unity of space. Through editing, messages can be conveyed, associations and oppositions created. Rapid cutting can give a sense of frenetic activity or confusion; slow cutting can give a sense of lingering nostalgia. Once one considers both the expressive potential of individual shots and the expressive potential of their combination, the artistic possibilities are practically limitless.[17]

Arnheim's work provides a fascinating account of the technical means to expression in silent film. It has its problems, however. Although we have not explored this here, Arnheim's arguments for why art should be expressive, what purpose artistic expression serves, and what it is for works of art to be expressive are plagued by ambiguity and inconsistency.[18] More relevant for us, however, is the restrictedness of his strategy for defending the art status of film. As we have seen, Arnheim locates the expressive potential of the film medium in discrepancies between the film image and perceived reality. This means that innovations for achieving greater realism in film merely reduce the chances of making film art. One such innovation is, of course, sound, which Arnheim flatly condemns. In fact, for several decades after the transition from silent to sound film, Arnheim continued to insist on the degeneracy of sound film. To think the opposite, that the introduction of sound is an improvement, 'is just as senseless as if the invention of three-dimensional oil painting were hailed as an advance on the hitherto known principles of painting'.[19]

Clearly something has gone wrong if Arnheim's approach requires us to denounce every sound film as artistically compromised. The historical explanation is of course that Arnheim was working against the assumption that film cannot be art because it is mere mechanical recording. Thus what he needed to emphasize were all the ways in which film fails to accurately reproduce reality. But to think only in terms of the limitations of film as a recording device is to miss the extra capacities of film as a representational art form. Instead of thinking of the introduction of sound as taking away from the expressive potential of the film medium, one can think of it as adding to the resources of the film-maker; giving her even more choices for how to tell a story, convey meaning and evoke emotions. Thinking about the sheer diversity of artistic resources available to the film-maker has led some contemporary philosophers to propose different kinds of argument for the independent art status of film. One such argument is made by Alexander Sesonske in a series of articles that focus on our unique experience of film.[20] There is much to remind us of Arnheim in Sesonske's work but whereas Arnheim distinguished film art technically, Sesonske distinguishes film art formally.

A CONTEMPORARY VIEW:
THE *EXTRA CAPACITIES* OF FILM MAKE IT AN ART

By the time that Sesonske is writing about film in the 1970s and 80s, the artistic possibilities of the medium have been widely acknowledged such that there is little danger of film being dismissed as mere mechanical recording. However, since new film media are also available by this time, questions arise about the advisability of relying on medium-specific arguments for film art. This could explain why Sesonke's account is formally rather than technically based – whether a film is shown on video or celluloid, many of its formal qualities will be the same. Moreover, film may no longer be dismissed as mere mechanical recording but that does not mean it has secured independent art status. In fact, as Sesonske describes, the tendency among filmmakers, film critics and film viewers is always to think of film in terms of some other established art form – for example, as visual poetry or recorded drama. The task for Sesonske is thus to find a way to understand and appreciate film on its own terms – in other words, to create an aesthetics of film. But where to begin?

The first step, according to Sesonske, in creating the aesthetics of any art form is an articulation of the range of formal possibilities inherent in the medium (or, perhaps, media).[21] Thus we can say that the defining formal dimensions of film are space, time and motion. Sound is important but not essential, since a film can be complete without sound. Film shares space with painting, sculpture and architecture, time with music, and motion with dance. You might think that film shares all its formal categories with drama. But space, time and motion are only integral to dramatic performance and not to the dramatic work itself, which is defined in terms of character and action.[22] Despite this distinction, however, the formal overlap between film and practically every other art form partly explains the tendency to think of it as a derivative art. But Sesonske insists that this is the wrong way of thinking. For every art form that has a formal category in common with another art form there are a unique range of formal possibilities within that category. Thus what film can *do* with space, time, and motion – how it represents them for us to experience[23] – is completely new. According to Sesonske, '[w]hen we view a film our experience of space, time, and motion differs from any other context of our lives'.[24]

Sesonske continues by arguing that the space and time we experience in film have a unique duality. Like the space of paintings, film space has a two-dimensional surface (of moving colours and forms) and a three-dimensional represented depth. But unlike painting-space the three-dimensional space of film is an 'action-space' in which motion can occur. This action-space is discontinuous both with real-life 'natural' space and with itself. We can have the sense of moving through a film's action-space while remaining in our seats in the Cinema. And both ourselves and the characters (though not usually in the fiction) can jump instantaneously from one location to another.

As well, however, we can jump from one point of time to another, thus indicating the parallel discontinuity of filmtime. While there is a particular length of time it takes to watch a film, there is also a particular length of time in which the events depicted on screen occur. The 'dramatic time' of represented events is more highly controlled than in any other art form, including literature: A prehistoric scene in a film can be immediately followed by a contemporary scene, or a segment of time in a continuous event can simply be cut out. This control is such that we may even experience a change in the form of time. For example, a freeze frame may be experienced, not merely as interrupted motion, but as though, in the world of the film, time itself has stopped.[25]

Despite these peculiarities, space and time in film do not feel that different to us. We may feel like we have seen an entire event even when only its highlights are shown on screen and, as Arnheim points out, we accept jumps in location as calmly as though we were turning the pages of a picture book. Indeed, it is often the sign of a good film that we fail to notice its unique treatment of space and time. Motion in film, however, is a different matter. Sesonske thinks that the way that motion in film is framed, edited and highlighted by camera angulation is hard to miss. The frame created by the screen gives motion a direction and magnitude that it lacks in real life; editing can give motion a new and aesthetically significant rhythm; and, camerawork can lend expressive force to even the tiniest movement. Moreover, given the discontinuity of film space, our relation to perceived motion in film has tremendous range: One moment we can see a movement on the distant horizon and in the next moment we can be engulfed and swept along by it through the world of the film.[26] If we think of a film like *Crouching Tiger, Hidden Dragon* (2000) with its swooping camerawork, it is easy to appreciate Sesonske's point here.

Thus Sesonske concludes with the following remark:

> In each of these formal categories, space, time, and motion, the modes that can be realized in cinema are unique to cinema. And though it is sometimes suggested that cinema must be inferior as an art because of its dependence on mechanical devices, we might note here that the creative possibilities in film are at least as great as in any art. As in literature, the whole of the world of the work is to be created, not only the characters and their actions but the very forms of space and time in which they act.[27]

CONCLUSIONS

The challenge in this chapter has been to show that despite what Sesonske describes as a 'dependence on mechanical devices,' film counts as an art form in its own right. It is not enough to show that film can incorporate aspects of traditional art forms, aspects like dramatization and painterly composition. Rather, it must be shown that film has its own methods for creating a world on screen for the viewer to enter in imagination.

Here is what we have covered in this chapter:

1. Scruton's sophisticated version of the 'canned-theatre' argument against film as an art form.
2. Two kinds of response to this argument; one which starts with King's defence of the art status of photography as the basis of film, and one

which draws upon Arnheim's detailed account of creative uses of the film medium.

3. Sesonske's further argument for film as an art form in terms of the formal possibilities inherent in its media.

Sesonke's argument shows us that we do not need to limit our attention to the traditional medium of film in order to uphold the art status of film. It is also worth noting that skeptical arguments like Scruton's which assume that film is at best a photograph of a dramatic representation cannot even get off the ground with films involving computer-generated imagery (CGI). When filmmakers employ CGI, they are not recording anything but instead doing something akin to painting. Indeed, CGI is most commonly used to depict scenes and entities that could not be recorded simply because they are fantastical or at least wholly fictional – for example, Aslan in Narnia or Gollum in Middle Earth. Even though CGI is usually used to create the illusion of reality – as though Aslan is part of the 'real' world caught on film, it still gives the filmmaker complete freedom over what to represent and how to represent it. Presumably, then, we can take an aesthetic interest in CGI. The skeptic might want to claim that films involving CGI are not really films. But since ordinary viewers and critics consider them to be films, this move reduces the skeptic's argument to an anachronistic and mainly verbal dispute about an early phase of filmmaking.[28]

CHAPTER 2

REALISM

In the previous chapter we were concerned with establishing that film is an art in its own right. The form of argument we considered emphasizes all the artistically significant ways in which film is not merely the mechanical recording of reality or theatre. In this form, the argument for film art leaves a key sceptical assumption untouched; namely, that mechanical recording cannot be art. Perhaps one could argue that film is a significant and distinct art form precisely because it involves mechanical recording. Then one would have to say what it is about filmrecording that has artistic significance. This may not be so difficult to do if one looks to the history of filmmaking.

In the late 1920s, a revolution occurred in filmmaking with the introduction of synchronous sound. Once the sound film was a technical (and commercial) possibility, there was no looking back; indeed, filmmakers and film-goers alike tended to assume that the introduction of sound represented a great improvement to the art form. Why would they assume this? If they were thinking like Rudolph Arnheim, after all, they would assume the opposite. As we know, Arnheim saw the introduction of sound as a further obstacle to creative expression which requires a divergence between film and reality. Given that sound film advocates did not share Arnheim's worries about sound, they must either have given up on film being art or have switched to a new film aesthetic. Thinking about some of the films made during this period – films like *Rules of the Game* (1939) and *Citizen Kane* (1941), convinces us that the latter and not the former possibility must be the case.

As usual, film theory was left to catch up with a filmmaking practice that embodied a new set of assumptions about the nature and value of film. Fortunately, one film theorist was paying close attention to the changing film world and understood the theoretical implications of the sound-film revolution. André Bazin, who began writing about film in the 1940s and continued until his death in 1959, is considered by many to be the most important figure in the history of film theory.[29] This is for two reasons: (1) Bazin was active as a film critic, historian and theorist during the most important period in the history of the film – the period in which sound film came into its own and established a new aesthetic of film; and (2) Bazin wrote about the films and film-makers of this period in a highly original, provocative and insightful way. The fundamental theoretical claim in his writings is that film is distinguished from other art forms by its distinctive capacity for realism, a capacity that derives from the nature of the filmmaking process. With the introduction of sound, film-makers came to recognize this capacity and exploit it in ever more refined ways.

Bazin's intuition about the distinct and supreme realism of film is widely shared. Even though some films and some film styles are considered more realistic than others, if you compare film to other art forms, it seems to stand out for its realism in a surprising way. To see what is surprising here, compare film and theatre: When you watch a play you are seeing real people – namely, actors – up on stage. When you watch a fiction film, on the other hand, you are merely seeing images of actors on a flat screen. Surely this implies that theatre is more realistic than film. And yet our intuitions point in a different direction as reflected in the tendency to describe some comparatively unrealistic films as 'theatrical'. Why is this? If we try to explain film realism in terms of the way cinematic portrayals are often particularly intimate, raw and affecting, we are merely going around in circles. For it would seem that the affective power of films is due in part to their realism and this is what we are trying to explain.

As we shall see, philosophers of film have tended to follow Bazin in trying to understand film realism in terms of the filmmaking process. The idea is that films are made up of photographs and photographs, as we learnt in Chapter 1, have a mechanical basis and thus a causal connection to their subjects. This connection is taken by different philosophers to imply different things. Kendall Walton takes it to imply that photographs are transparent – we see their objects through them.[30] Gregory Currie, on the other hand, who is one of several critics of Walton, takes the casual connection to imply that photographic and cinematographic images are in a class of representations that also includes such natural signs as tree rings and footprints but excludes paintings and drawings.[31] To see what is appealing about each of these views, we need to consider them as part of a long debate that began with Bazin in the 1940s, suffered an extended interruption during the heyday of psycho-semiotic film theory, and then recently reignited among analytic philosophers with interests in perception and the mind more generally.

In a way it is surprising that the contemporary argument about film realism still focuses on the photographic basis of film given that the traditional medium of film is fast being replaced by digital formats. It is an open question, therefore, as to how one would defend the realism of digital film. Insofar as digital images can be as much mechanical recording as celluloid photographs, some traditional arguments for film realism may still be applicable. But this will only be in a limited way given that digital images can also be endlessly manipulated.

It is worth noting that digital films in which extensive manipulation is obvious – if only because the films portray fictional locations and fictional entities – can still be considered highly realistic. Perhaps this is a hold-over from the days of photographically-based film: Perhaps, at some level, we still tend to think of film, the art form, in terms of film, the photographic medium. On the other hand, it might suggest that the realism of film images had nothing to do with their causal history in the first place.

Another limitation of arguments for film realism that start with the photograph is that they have little to say about the realistic contribution of one seemingly essential[32] and distinctive feature of film; namely, motion. Now that film is a multi-media art form, the impression of motion on the screen can be created in a variety of ways. When film involves a celluloid film strip, however, this impression is created by rapidly running a series of static photographic frames through a projector. In light of this method for creating apparent motion, a debate has sprung up among philosophers as to whether the motion we see on screen is a straightforward illusion or in some sense real. Perhaps it seems obvious to you that films do not really move. But the obviousness of this conclusion may be an important clue to understanding our entrenched and largely unquestioned ways of thinking about film realism.

BAZIN: THE FILM IMAGE *IS* THE OBJECT

In a series of essays collected in *What is Cinema?*[33] Bazin defends realism in two stages. First, he examines the nature of the film image – its mechanical production and causal connection to the object – in order to show that realism is the essence of film art. Then he argues that a particular style of filmmaking is *the* realist style. This is the style that Jean Renoir perfected in the 1930s with films like *Rules of the Game*. It is also the style of several post-war American directors, including Orson

Welles and Billy Wilder, and Italian neorealists like Vittorio De Sica and Roberto Rossellini. We will review the defining characteristics of this style in a moment, but before we do, we need to consider the intelligibility of Bazin's approach. If he is going to argue that film by its very nature is realistic, thereby implying that any film in any style would be realistic, how can Bazin also try to isolate a particular realist film style? The way Bazin tries to do this is by claiming that the style of Renoir, Welles, *et al.* is the style that most fully realizes the natural purpose of the traditional film medium. Given the mechanical basis of filmmaking, this purpose is to 're-present' reality in an 'objective' and thus insightful way. There are, however, problems with what Bazin is trying to do here. These will become clear as we examine his view in more detail.

The so-called realist style that emerged in the films of Renoir is in many ways the same style used in mainstream film today, although technical innovations have rendered the style gradually more transparent over time. Among its characteristics are the following: (1) The use of medium-long shots – shots in which the whole of an actor's body is visible on screen, often with space above his head; (2) the use of deep focus techniques as opposed to the soft focus techniques of 1930s Hollywood films; (3) the composition of shots with dramatic details located on different pictorial planes rather than concentrated in the foreground; (4) the use of the long take to capture a whole scene instead of breaking it down into several shots; (5) the use of camera movement instead of editing to follow the action; and, (6) a non-theatrical, non-painterly use of the frame as a result of the camera following the action.[34]

All of these characteristics are evident in the style of *Rules of the Game* though not all of them in every shot. And though there are important differences in narrative structure and subject-matter between Renoir, the Italian neorealists, and the American post-war directors, they share a commitment to the use of sequence shots in continuous space and thus an opposition to the highly interventionist techniques of montage. But why does Bazin think that this style and no other is realistic? The reason is that he thinks this style comes closest to a simple recording of what is going on in front of the camera. If the actors' performances are captured in a single long take with a moving camera, rather than in a series of edited shots, the natural unity of space and continuity of time is preserved. The moving camera also gives the action a feeling of independence – as though the camera is simply following what happens instead of framing a staged scene. Finally, and perhaps most importantly, the use of deep focus photography enables the viewer to scan the recorded scene for interesting details just as she scans her surroundings in real life. The overall perceptual experience of a Renoir film is therefore closer to ordinary perceptual experience precisely because the recording aspect of the medium is emphasized.

This marks a transitional point in Bazin's argument – the point at which he identifies his favoured film style with the essence of film art. Recall that for Arnheim, the essentially cinematic qualities of particular films are their expressive qualities, and these qualities are the result of medium-specific divergences from mechanical recording. For Bazin, in direct contrast, the essentially cinematic qualities of particular films are their reproductive or presentational qualities, and these qualities result directly from mechanical recording. Indeed, it is the mechanical basis of film that raises the art form in its original medium above the traditional representational arts: Whereas a representational painting, for example, only stands in for reality, a film or a photograph *retrieves* reality. Bazin explains this rather strange idea in the following way:

> The objective nature of photography confers on it a quality of credibility absent from all other picture-making. In spite of any objections our critical spirit may offer, we are forced to accept as real the existence of the object reproduced, actually *re*-presented, set before us, that is to say, in time and space. Photography enjoys a certain advantage in virtue of this transference of reality from the thing to its reproduction.[35]

Bazin then goes even further with the following claim: 'The photographic image is the object itself, the object freed from the conditions of time and space that govern it'.[36] What could Bazin mean here given that we usually have no difficulty distinguishing between a photograph and the thing photographed? Perhaps we should take it as mere hyperbole or metaphor and assume that Bazin is simply trying to emphasize the difference between the photographic arts and the traditional representational arts. Taking the claim literally, after all, would seem to commit us to a doubtful metaphysics – one that allows for the identity of things which are clearly not one and the same; namely, a photograph of something and the thing itself. Perhaps, though, Bazin's claim is to be taken literally once it is more fully spelt out. From some of his other remarks, it is plausible to take Bazin to mean that the way in which the image and its object are identical is akin to the way in which two casts from the same mold are identical. Alternatively, it is also plausible to take Bazin to mean that the image and object are identical insofar as they produce the same image on the retina. These interpretations are certainly possible but they need to be explained and their implications explored.

Just as the static photograph re-presents a moment of reality, so the 'moving' film image, on Bazin's account, re-presents a segment of reality with a particular duration:

> Viewed in this perspective, the cinema is objectivity in time. The film is no longer content to preserve the object, enshrouded as it were in an instant, as the bodies of insects are preserved intact, out of the distant past, in amber. . . . Now for the first time, the image of things is likewise the image of their duration, change mummified as it were.[37]

At this point, one might begin to wonder if, by focusing on the recording aspect of the medium, Bazin has not so much succeeded in defending film as the supremely realistic art form, but rather, has succeeded in confirming the suspicions of those who want to deny that film is any kind of art form. After all, mechanical recording, even if it is facilitated creatively, is not in itself either creative or expressive. It might seem, therefore, that either Bazin has to give up his account of film realism or he has to give up on film's claim to art status. But, not surprisingly, he does neither. Rather, he works with different assumptions about the nature of art in order to claim that film is art precisely because it is inherently realistic. Interestingly, however, it seems that realism is an aesthetic value for Bazin for some of the same reasons that expressiveness is an aesthetic value for Arnheim: A highly realistic visual artwork just like an expressive visual artwork gives us a new way of seeing the world:

> The aesthetic qualities of photography are to be sought in its power to lay bare the realities. It is not for me to separate off, in the complex fabric of the objective world, here a reflection on a damp sidewalk, there the gesture of a child. Only the impassive lens, stripping its object of all those ways of seeing it, those piled-up preconceptions, that spiritual dust and grime with which the eyes have covered it, is able to present it in all its virginal purity to my attention and consequently to my love.[38]

As we have already mentioned, Bazin wants to derive a particular film style from his account of the nature of the film image. But it is not clear how he can do this without contradiction. Given his claim that the photographic process necessarily results in images that re-present reality, Bazin has surely committed himself to describing as realistic any film in any style that is made in the usual, photographic way. Indeed, Bazin himself seems to realize this commitment when he claims that no matter how distorted or fuzzy a photographic image, 'it shares, by virtue of the very process of its becoming, the being of the model of which it is the reproduction'.[39] If Bazin will allow that fuzzy shots are realistic, why not highly expressionistic or otherwise stylized ones? However, just as with his rather extravagant claim that the image is the object, there may be a way to interpret Bazin's attempted derivation more moderately: Perhaps Bazin's point is just that, since our experience of films in the style of Renoir, Welles, *et al.* reproduces our ordinary perceptual experience in some respects more closely than earlier styles like Soviet montage and German expressionism, the style of Renoir, Welles, *et al.* better expresses the inherent realism of the medium. This is not an implausible suggestion even though Bazin does not support it with a fully developed argument.

As we shall see, the idea that film and photography are realistic because their manner of production supports a certain kind of perceptual experience is taken up by the philosopher, Kendall Walton. Walton provides the argument that Bazin needed, avoiding both metaphysical absurdity and contradiction, though, as his several critics will tell us, there is still something a little strange about his claims. Just as we may balk at Bazin's claim that the object is the image, we may balk at Walton's claim that we see the object through the image.

Before we come to Walton, however, there is one other criticism of Bazin's account worth mentioning. The criticism concerns the application of his account to fiction films. As Noël Carroll points out,[40] given that film images re-present their objects, Bazin is committed to saying that their subjects are always real. Thus, in the case of a fiction film, Bazin can only talk about the film re-presenting actors and sets rather than characters in fictional settings. But this is surely a strange way of talking given that what is most relevant to our viewing of a fiction film is that it represents certain characters. In addition, it is not as though the category of fiction films is a minor or marginal one; on the contrary, the bulk of films most of us watch, and indeed the bulk of films that are made, are fictional narratives. And Bazin himself spends most of his time with fiction films. Yet he does not have an account of the way that the real object allegedly re-presented by the film image can also stand in for or nominally portray something fictional.

Once more, however, Walton comes to the rescue. He suggests that in our experience of fiction films, it is actually the case that we see the actors through the photographs projected on screen, but it is also fictionally the case that we see the characters. In other words, we actually see the actors, albeit indirectly, but we imagine seeing the characters. If a fiction film is filmed on location rather than in a studio, it is both actually and fictionally the case that we see the scene of the story. This explains why some filmmakers aim to give their works of fiction the quality of home movies or documentaries – say, by using hand-held cameras and only natural lighting. This stylistic choice emphasizes the recording aspect of the medium and, consequently, may make it easier to imagine that you are seeing the characters, rather than just the actors, through the film. Thus, on Walton's view, fiction films can function on different levels, both realistically and imaginatively. Whether or not this solution is a good one, however, it is not a solution that is available to Bazin. On his view, the image just is the object, and insofar as the object is not a fictional portrayal of anything, neither is the image.

A related worry will emerge later in the chapter with Gregory Currie's response to Walton. As we shall see, Currie is concerned that Walton's argument for transparency is just like Bazin's in that it takes photographs out of the category of representations altogether. Even though Walton addresses this concern in a response to Currie, it is interesting that it keeps re-emerging whenever the causal relation between a photograph and its object is emphasized. You may remember from Chapter 1 that Roger Scruton had exactly the same concern and was quite adamant that true photographs, given their mechanical basis, cannot represent. The challenge, therefore, is to find a way to acknowledge the importance of the photographic process for an account of film realism and, at the same time, account for the realism of fiction films as fictions.

WALTON: THE FILM IMAGE IS TRANSPARENT

Like us, Walton is interested in what is behind Bazin's confusing claim that the photographic image is the object. Thus he is interested in the idea that photographs are realistic by their very nature, in virtue of having been made in a certain way. This idea seems right to Walton and serves as a starting point for his account of the transparency of photographs. Walton agrees with Bazin that photographs are not realistic in virtue of their appearance or in virtue of their accuracy. Even a fuzzy or distorted photograph is realistic on their views, and in a way that a painting cannot be no matter how naturalistic or illusionistic.

Thus it is suggested that there is a fundamental gap between photography and painting in terms of realism. A point that is often made much of in establishing this gap is that paintings can be of things that do not exist whereas photographs cannot be. Walton and Currie, however, both think that this point is not that significant. Currie suspects that it is mere prejudice to say that a painting that uses a model to represent Saint Anne, for example, is a painting of Saint Anne but a comparable photograph that also uses a model is not thereby a photograph of Saint Anne but only a photograph of a model representing Saint Anne.[41] Walton, on the other hand, points out that even when a painting is of something actual, it cannot be as realistic as a photograph. His example is a painted portrait compared to a photographic portrait of Abraham Lincoln: Why, Walton asks, is the latter more realistic than the former?[42]

The answer, Walton thinks, is that we quite literally see Lincoln through the photograph but not through the painting. In other words, when we look at the photograph of Lincoln, while we recognize it as a photograph, we nevertheless see through it as we see through such things as eye glasses and microscopes. We do not merely have the impression of seeing Lincoln, nor do we actually just see a duplicate of Lincoln. Rather than being a way of gaining access to something that we cannot see, the photograph of Lincoln is a way of indirectly seeing what we cannot see directly. Thus a photograph is like eyeglasses and microscopes both in its transparency and also in being an aid to vision. But, you may ask, how can a photograph allow us to see Lincoln when he is dead? In other words, how can a photograph allow us to see into the past? Recall that Bazin confronted this issue when he claimed that the photographic image is the object 'freed from the conditions of time and space that govern it'.[43] In other words, on Bazin's view, a photograph preserves or 'mummifies' an object at a particular moment in its existence so that it is always available to us as long as the photograph exists. Walton does not want to say that an object from the past is literally brought forward into the present by a photograph. But he is quite comfortable with the idea that we see into the past when we see an object through a photograph. This is not because he relies on some special sense of 'seeing' – he takes himself to be using the ordinary sense throughout his discussion – but because he establishes important analogies between other forms of indirect seeing and our experience of photographs.

The way that Walton does this is by using a slippery slope argument that gives his transparency claim 'initial plausibility'. First Walton asserts that no one will deny that we see through eyeglasses, mirrors, and telescopes. How, he then asks, could someone deny that a security guard also sees via closed circuit television or a sports fan sees via a live television broadcast? But after going this far, surely we can also speak of seeing athletic events via delayed broadcasts. The difference is that now we're seeing events in the past. But Walton is not sure this difference matters. After all, we talk of seeing the explosion of a star that occurred millions of years ago through a high-powered telescope. The question is whether any of the differences on the slide down the slippery slope are enough to mark a theoretical distinction between seeing and not seeing something.[44] Walton thinks that we cannot justifiably stop the slide before we get to photographs, and photographs are at the bottom of the slope. However, some of Walton's critics dig their heels in on the slippery slope by specifying conditions for seeing that photographs fail to satisfy. We will turn to the challenge of the slippery slope in the next section. First we need to consider Walton's necessary and sufficient conditions for transparency.

According to Walton, the reason that we can see through photographs is that they are caused by their objects in a mechanical way.[45] Although the photographer can play an important role in determining what we see through her photographs, we nevertheless see through them as a result of a mechanical process that preserves the necessary causal relation for perceptual contact. As a result of this causal relation, the appearance of a photograph is 'counterfactually dependent' on the appearance of the object photographed. This means that the photograph would have looked different if the object had looked different. Counterfactual dependence can also be preserved without such a causal relation, however. Lincoln's painted portrait might also have looked different if Lincoln looked different. But this is the result of a change in the painter's beliefs mediating the relation between the painting and its object. If Lincoln had looked different to the painter, then the painter would have painted Lincoln looking different. Unless, of course, the painter is not really seeing what Lincoln looks like because the painter is hallucinating. Then the appearance of the painting will not reliably depend on the appearance of its subject. With the photographic portrait of Lincoln, however, even if the photographer were hallucinating, the appearance of the photograph will reliably depend on Lincoln's appearance. To sum up, photographs are transparent because they are caused by their objects and thus exhibit counterfactual dependence which is not mediated by beliefs. Currie helpfully calls this kind of counterfactual dependence, 'natural dependence', in contrast to the 'intentional dependence' exhibited by paintings of actual things.[46]

The next question to consider is whether natural dependence is a necessary and sufficient condition for transparency. Walton defends the necessity of natural dependence with the imagined case of blind Helen who is fitted with a prosthetic device through which a neurosurgeon feeds her visual experiences. Walton thinks that our intuitions tell us that blind Helen is not seeing through her prosthesis because her visual experiences are mediated by the neurosurgeon's beliefs. Even if the neurosurgeon is completely trustworthy and makes every effort to feed Helen accurate information, Walton thinks this does not count as a case of seeing. It is worth noting, however, that the intuitive force of this case may not be as strong as Walton thinks. Currie, for one, thinks that Helen is seeing through her prosthesis precisely because the neurosurgeon is trustworthy. Imagine instead, Currie suggests, that it is an omnipotent and omnibenevolent god that feeds all of us our visual experiences. Even though our visual experiences are mediated in this case, could we not still say that we see, thanks to the complete reliability of our source of visual experiences?

Leaving this question aside, Walton comes up himself with a case that shows that natural dependence is not sufficient, on its own, for transparency. He asks us to imagine a machine which is sensitive to the light reflected by an object such that it accurately records the object, but as a verbal description rather than as a picture. In this case, the machine's print-out is caused mechanically by the object and would have been different if the object were different. The print-out thus exhibits natural dependency. But, Walton concedes, the machine's print-out is surely not transparent.[47]

This case leads Walton to propose another condition with which natural dependency is jointly sufficient for transparency: the preservation of real similarity relations. To see what this condition consists in, consider again the description-generating machine. Walton decides that the reason that this machine's print-out is not transparent is that it supports a different kind of discrimination than the kind supported by ordinary perception of the object described. The best way to see this is to compare the kinds of errors we are prone to make about the description and about the object described. Let's say the description is of a house. In ordinary perceptual experience, it may be easy to mistake a house for a barn. But in reading the description of the house, this is not the kind of mistake we are likely to make. With the description, it is much more likely that we will mistake the house for a hearse because the words 'house' and 'hearse' look similar. With a photograph of the house, on the other hand, we are likely to make the barn mistake and not the hearse mistake. In other words, we are likely to make the same kind of mistake as we make in ordinary perceptual experience. The kind of discrimination supported by the photograph establishes the same kind of similarities and differences as in ordinary perception. And, according to Walton, a 'process of discrimination counts as perceptual only if its structure is thus analogous to the structure of the world. When we perceive, we are in this way, intimate with what is perceived'. We cannot see through the mechanical description because discriminating between words for things is crucially unlike discriminating between the things themselves.[48]

Thus, on Walton's view, the transparency of photographs must be distinguished from the opacity of both paintings and descriptions. A painting may be counterfactually dependent on its object but only via someone's beliefs about the object. Thus a painting does not satisfy the condition of *natural* counterfactual dependence. A mechanical description, on the other hand, exhibits natural dependence and thus has what Walton considers necessary – depending on the intuitive force of the case of blind Helen – for transparency. But since we cannot, in fact, see through the description, natural dependence must not be sufficient on its own for transparency. The further condition for transparency that Walton introduces – the preservation of real similarity relations – is perhaps not that easy to grasp, in part because it is not that easy to compare modes of discrimination. As Walton's critics point out,[49] it may be that some but not all of the errors we are likely to make when looking at a certain kind of representation are the same as the errors we make in ordinary perceptual experience. Then the question becomes, how much discriminatory overlap is enough to establish the transparency of a certain kind of representation over another kind.

In response to this question, Currie provides a case involving two clocks, A and B, designed to show that natural dependence and the preservation of real similarity relations are not jointly sufficient for transparency. The orientation of clock A's hands governs the orientation of clock B's hands by means of a radio signal. Thus there is a natural dependence between my visual experience of clock B and the appearance of clock A such that any errors I make in perceiving B, I would also make in perceiving A. But if clock A were out of sight and I were just looking at B, there is no plausibility to the claim that I am seeing clock A when I look at clock B. In this case, even though there is complete discriminatory overlap, such that clock B undoubtedly preserves real similarity relations with clock A while being naturally dependent on clock A, there is no transparency. Whether or not we are convinced by this case, the use of counterexamples more generally represents one popular kind of critical response to Walton. Clearly it is time to consider more closely the overall structure of the critical debate surrounding Walton's account.

WALTON'S CRITICS: THE FILM IMAGE IS *NOT* TRANSPARENT

The controversial nature of Walton's claim that we literally see through photographs has motivated close critical attention to his argument. The resulting debate can be initially characterized in terms of two general responses to Walton's slippery slope argument. The first response involves taking up the challenge to find theoretically significant differences between photographs and other things that we can agree we see through, like mirrors, eyeglasses, and microscopes. In this way, critics try to stop the slide down Walton's slippery slope. The second response also involves stopping the slide but stopping it before it starts. A critic can refuse to take the first step onto the slippery slope by denying that we see through mirrors, eyeglasses, microscopes, telescopes and television footage. Then a comparison between these things and photographs will not yield the conclusion that photographs are transparent.

There are at least two forms that such a refusal has taken in the literature. Gregory Currie effectively refuses to step on to the slippery slope when he gives an account of pictorial representation that would seem to apply to mirrors.[50] If mirrors are representations, on Currie's view, then we do not see through them. But mirrors are close to the top of Walton's slippery slope – something that we can supposedly all agree we see through. More generally, Jonathan Friday refuses to step onto the slippery slope when he defends a theory of perception that rules out any form of indirect seeing.[51] On the direct realist theory of perception, we cannot be said to see through any device, be it a mirror, a microscope, or a photograph. The further challenge for those critics, like Currie and Friday, who refuse Walton's challenge of stopping the slide down the slippery slope once it has started is to account for why it is that we nevertheless have the sense that we see through such things as mirrors and microscopes. Friday attempts to give an error theory[52] to explain this sense and criticizes Currie for failing to do likewise.

There are a number of suggestions for theoretically significant differences between photographs and the various devices that precede them on Walton's slippery slope. Although we can only briefly mention them here, they are all worth closer consideration. The general aim with these suggestions is to show that, just because we think that we see through mirrors, telescopes and the like, we are not thereby committed to thinking that we also see through photographs. Edwin Martin suggests two differences that might stop the slide: the difference between real and virtual images,[53] and the comparative length of the causal chain between the object of perception and the medium of perception. Nigel Warburton gives four conditions for seeing that photographs fail to satisfy.[54] These are 'virtual simultaneity' between what is seen and our seeing it, 'temporal congruity' between the duration of our visual experience and the duration of the event that we experience, the sensitivity of our visual experience to changes in what we experience, and knowledge of what caused us to have a certain visual experience such that we can position ourselves in relation to what we see. There are, however, ways of challenging the relevance of all of these differences.

Walton himself gives counterexamples that effectively undermine Martin's conditions for seeing. The case of the compound microscope, the lower lens of which produces a real image seen through the upper lens, shows that seeing need not only involve virtual images. The case of a series of 10,000 mirrors arranged to relay light from the object to the viewer shows that the length of the causal chain need not affect seeing – that is, as long as one thinks that we can at least see through one mirror. In response to Warburton, Jonathan Friday suggests that Warburton's conditions for seeing are not obviously essential to seeing. Virtual simultaneity may not be essential depending on how we interpret a case Friday imagines that involves adding a delay function to a prosthesis which facilitates sight. The conditions of temporal congruity and sensitivity to change only apply to the seeing of events and not to the seeing of objects. And, finally, in relation to Warburton's fourth condition, Friday suggests that it may be sufficient for seeing to know that there is a causal link between our visual experience and its object without having the kind of knowledge of the causal process that would allow us to position ourselves in relation to the object.

These arguments deserve closer attention than we can give them here. But the way is still open for others to take up the challenge of stopping the slide down Walton's slippery slope. Perhaps there are other significant ways in which photographs are unlike those devices that we agree we see through. At present, however, it appears that Walton's slope is even more slippery than his critics have assumed. Given just how slippery, perhaps it is best not to step onto the slope in the first place. This brings us to Currie's classification of photographs as natural representations. Currie agrees with Walton's emphasis on the difference between what Currie calls the natural counterfactual dependence of photographs and the intentional counterfactual dependence of paintings. Whereas the appearance of a painting of something actual depends on the appearance of that thing only insofar as the painter's beliefs are similarly dependent, the appearance of a photograph depends on the appearance of its object regardless of what the photographer believes.

Walton can try to use this distinction to ground the transparency of photographs because our ordinary perceptual experiences exhibit the same natural dependency as photographs. However, as we have seen, Currie thinks that the argument for transparency fails because Walton is unable to successfully specify necessary and sufficient conditions for transparency. This failure simply confirms Currie's sense that the difference between natural and intentional dependency does not mark a difference between seeing things and merely seeing pictures of things. Rather, it marks out two categories of representations. In the category of 'natural' representations we find photographs, but also natural signs like tree rings and footprints. In the category of 'intentional' representations we find drawings and paintings. Photographs and paintings may be different kinds of representation, and this is important to realize, but as representations, both photographs and paintings stand in for things; they do not mediate our seeing of things.

Interestingly, Walton claims that, in fact, he does not mean to deny that photographs are representations.[55] As representations, photographs function to generate imagined perceptual contact with fictional characters and events. Walton insists that his point is that photographs are representations that we also see through. This of course raises the question of whether representations, particularly pictures, are the kind of thing that one can see through (to their objects). Currie seems to assume they are not when he argues that photographs are natural representations, not transparencies. But what we really need here is a theory of pictorial representation or depiction. In the next section, we shall see how Currie derives a particular explanation of film realism from just such a theory.

Friday suggests that what makes Walton's slippery slope so slippery is a particular kind of causal theory of perception; namely a representationalist causal theory of perception. For the representationalist, ordinary seeing is mediated by a mental representation whereas for the direct realist, ordinary seeing is essentially unmediated. Furthermore, for the representationalist, the difference between what counts as seeing and what is mere hallucination depends on the relation between the mental representations we see through and the things we see through them. And this relation is just the kind that Walton insists upon for transparency; namely, a relation of natural counterfactual dependence. Thus we can see why representationalism might be the lubricant for Walton's slippery slope: As Friday explains, 'if there is no objection to saying that we see through mental pictures that meet certain conditions, why should we object to the claim that we can see through physical intermediaries that meet the same conditions?'[56]

The issue for Friday is that representationalist theories of perception have been widely discredited and replaced by direct realist theories. But direct realist theories do not allow for seeing in virtue of any mediators, mental or physical. Thus the direct realist does not step onto the Walton's slippery slope. There is, however, according to Friday, a cost associated with resisting the slippery slope. The cost is having to explain our intuition that we see through such things as mirrors, microscopes, and indeed, photographs, even though, according to the realist, our intuition is mistaken. Friday accepts this cost and argues that the intuition is the result of our confusing a new way of seeing with a new attitude towards what is seen. (This is Friday's error theory, mentioned earlier.) In light of the way that photographs are produced, we tend to take a practical attitude towards them as means of discovering their objects. In other words, we treat photographs as though they give us direct perceptual contact to their objects when we treat them as evidence, proof of presence or as windows onto past events.[57] We may treat photographs as though they are transparent but that does not mean they really are transparent.

CURRIE: THE FILM IMAGE IS HIGHLY DEPICTIVE

So far we have considered two explanations of the distinctive realism of films and photographs. Bazin's explanation is that a photograph literally puts us in the presence of its object. Walton's explanation is that we literally see the object through the photograph. Both of these explanations mark a fundamental divide between photographs and other kinds of pictures on the basis of their distinct modes of production. Currie's explanation, on the other hand, is an explanation of the realism of pictures in general, or, more specifically, an explanation of what makes depiction, the distinctive way in which pictures represent, distinctly realistic. The degree to which a representational work of art is realistic depends on how much it depicts rather than represents in some other way – say, linguistically. What distinguishes film realism, on this account, is the 'depictive potential' of film media. Other kinds of visual art can depict states of affairs but only film can also depict time and space. In other words, films can be more thoroughly realistic than other kinds of representational art because they can represent more of the world realistically. But what makes depiction so realistic?

Currie's account of depiction is based on a particular theory of mind and an attention to what is going on with the viewer. On this account, when a picture depicts an object, we employ the same recognitional capacities in relation to the depiction as we would in relation to the object itself.[58] The likeness between a horse and a picture of a horse, for example, is one of appearance whereby the horse and the picture share properties significant for our recognition of horses – the horse and the picture trigger the same recognitional capacity.[59] Of course there are many properties that a picture of a horse has that a horse doesn't have (flatness, for example), and vice versa. But all that matters is that the horse and the horse picture share the property (or set of properties) that triggers the horse recognitional capacity, whatever that property may be.

When the picture triggers your horse-recognitional capacity this does not mean that you think there is a horse in front of you.[60] Your horse-recognitional capacity is a different kind of mental operation than rational judgment – Currie describes the capacity as a 'quick-and-dirty mechanism which, somewhere deep in my visual-processing system, identifies a certain input as a horse'. In other words, it is a more automatic and less flexible process that works, 'not on the basis of a detailed, comprehensive examination of the visual input in the light of background belief and all the rest, but on the basis of just a few clues extracted from the visual input itself'.[61] It is, however, precisely because my horse-recognitional capacity is the kind of mental operation it is that depiction works as it does. Because my horse-recognitional capacity is quick-and-dirty, it can be fooled by things like donkeys at dusk and stuffed horses, but particularly by horse pictures.

Thus depiction is an essentially realistic form of representation because it works by exploiting our visual capacities to recognize the objects depicted. And film, according to Currie, is the art form that uses depiction most pervasively and naturally. This is seen best with the aesthetically significant decision to depict, rather than represent in some other way, spatial and temporal relations between objects as well as the objects themselves. A film depicts time and space when it uses the temporal and spatial properties of its elements to represent the temporal and spatial properties of the things represented. A succession of events, for example, can be represented by the length of time it takes to observe them on screen and the order in which they are experienced on screen. And the height of a six-foot man on screen can be represented by his being a determinate height in relation to the other characters and the scene as a whole.

Even though depiction is not the only way to represent space and time, it is the default in film. A film-maker could decide to represent the passage of time with a fade, with a dissolve or with the words 'twenty years later' suddenly appearing on the screen.[62] But in the absence of such devices, we assume that the time it takes to represent an event is the time the event itself takes. If it takes 5 minutes to represent a conversation, we assume the conversation lasts 5 minutes. That is, unless the conversation is obviously broken up, perhaps by being intercut with other scenes.

Currie can then explain why Bazin took the style of filmmakers like Renoir, which involves long-take, deep-focus photography, to be inherently realistic. This is because Renoir's style enhances our ability to detect the spatial and temporal properties of a film scene by using the natural capacity we have to detect those properties of things in the real world.[63] Deep focus, in particular, allows us to shift our attention at will from one object on screen to another, just as we are able to do in the real world. With montage style, on the other hand, quick cutting between distinct spatial and temporal perspectives requires us to judge spatial and temporal properties by means of inference from the overall dramatic structure of the film. Currie is thus able to show, with a coherent and plausible account of depiction, that Bazin was really onto something when he interpreted the aesthetic significance of introducing sound to film in terms of realism.

DOES THE FILM IMAGE REALLY MOVE?

Perhaps so far in this discussion of film realism, you have felt there is something missing. In moving seamlessly from the analysis of photographs to the analysis of film images, we have not drawn attention to the fact that film has extra capacities for realism that photography lacks. The most obvious of these capacities is the capacity for depicting motion. Whereas a photograph might capture a kung-fu fighter frozen in mid-air, a film can capture the kung-fu fighter's entire balletic trajectory. Perhaps Bazin's description of the way film 'mummifies' change fails to do justice to the dynamic quality of the art form – just as our world is full of movement, so are the worlds of film. We can follow the kung-fu fighter's moves because the image moves – or does it?

If the kung-fu fighter's leap is captured in a single shot from a fixed perspective, we can assume that the actor playing the kung-fu fighter really moved before the camera. But if we are watching the kung-fu film in a cinema, the movement we see on the screen is traditionally generated by the projection of 24 static frames per second.[64] Knowing this, we might say that the traditional projection mechanism for photographically-based film merely creates an illusion of motion for creatures with our particular perceptual apparatus. In other words, the answer to the question in this section's title – 'does the film image really move?' – is straightforwardly, 'no'.

But perhaps this answer is not so straightforward. Currie[65] and Noël Carroll[66] are fully aware of the static mechanical basis of the impression of motion in film, and yet they suggest that the film image really does move just because it moves for us. While this does not mean that film motion is real in some ultimate, metaphysical sense, it does mean that film motion is not an illusion. In the same way, colours perceived under the right conditions are not illusory even if they are merely apparent. If colours were always illusory, we could not make sense of the fact that we distinguish special cases of the illusion of colour.[67] We can be right and wrong about what colour something really is because we take the real colour of something to be the colour it appears to normal viewers under normal viewing conditions. This is why colours are commonly referred to as real, response-dependent properties. Currie and Carroll think that film motion is real in the same way because normal viewers under normal film-viewing conditions really see the film image move.

Currie does not think he has to give a positive argument for his view because the burden of proof is on those who distrust our experience of film motion when, in general, we should start out by trusting our perceptual experiences.[68] Currie therefore proceeds by attempting to undermine the opposing view. Specifically, he challenges two common arguments for 'illusionism,' the commonsense view that motion in film is an illusion.

On the first argument, the motion of film images is an illusion because when we look at the film strip apart from the projector, there is no motion; there is just a series of still negative images. Both Currie and Carroll have a ready response to this argument: The illusion that is up for debate is the illusion of motion on the screen, not on the film strip. It is the film engaged by the projector that appears to move. Consider the analogous case of musical recordings: If we hold an audio CD up to our ear, we don't hear any music. But that does not mean that the music we hear when we play the CD on our stereo is an illusion.

The second argument for illusionism that Currie considers points to the fact that it is specifically creatures like us that see motion on the screen. On a scientifically objective description, the film projection process is just a matter of light particles hitting the screen. We could also give an objective description of the way that the projection apparatus engages the human perceptual apparatus. But movement only enters in when we describe the subjective experience that consistently results from this engagement. Thus only a subjective and not an objective description of the film projection process involves motion. But Currie also has a ready response to this argument: All that the argument indicates is that film motion is a real, response-dependent property like colour.

Currie then considers a compelling objection to his own proposal; namely, that it destroys the distinction between the real and the merely apparent, eliminating many or perhaps all illusions. Consider the famous Müller-Lyer illusion, which involves two horizontal lines of equal length, the top one with an outward-pointing arrowhead at each end and the bottom one with an inward-pointing arrowhead at each end:

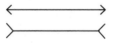

The illusion we have when we look at these lines is that the bottom line is longer than the top line. But, on Currie's account, couldn't we say that the greater length of the inward-pointing-arrows line is a real, response-dependent property? After all, none of us can help but see the greater length, given the kind of perceptual apparatus we have. If we accept Currie's proposal, couldn't we say that anything we perceive is real in a response-dependent way – the mirage shimmering in the desert, the way that film characters seem to approach us when we are watching a film with 3D glasses, or the way that water in waves seems to move towards us on the beach?

Currie says 'no'. Our intuitions tell us that there is an important difference between genuine illusions like the Müller-Lyer illusion and the phenomenon of film motion. The reason the Müller-Lyer illusion is a genuine illusion is because the misleading appearance of the two lines can be undermined by a simple and readily available 'independent check' – say, by measurement with an ordinary ruler or even with a piece of string. By contrast, Currie thinks that the ordinary film viewer cannot check whether he is really seeing motion on the screen. This is because our experience is of images, and not physical objects, moving on screen, and there is no way to check the movement of images independently of our experience of them.[69]

Andrew Kania objects to this response, however. Surely, he counters, there is an independent test for the illusion of film motion: Simply by slowing down the projector, the viewer can see, with the naked eye, the static projected frames go by, one by one.[70] Moreover, to object that this merely alters the conditions required for the impression of motion misses the point. Kania argues that the point is not to claim that since you don't see motion on screen when the projector is slowed down, it must be an illusion that you see motion on screen when the projector runs at normal speed. This would not convince anyone, just as it would not convince anyone that the Müller-Lyer illusion is not an illusion if you covered the arrowheads so that we no longer see a difference in the length of the two lines. Instead, the point of slowing down the projector is to bring someone to an understanding of what is going on at a lower, mechanical level so that she changes her mind about what is going on when the projector operates at normal speed.[71]

To this, a Curriean might respond by invoking the case of solidity from the history of science. When scientists discovered that nothing is solid in the way we thought – that is, nothing is thoroughly homogeneous, they didn't conclude that tables, chairs and bars of gold are not solid. Analogously, it is not clear that we should deny motion to films just because we know that their underlying bases do not exactly move.[72]

But Kania insists that this is a bad analogy. In the case of solidity, paradigmatic cases were examined and it was found that *nothing* is solid in the way we thought. However, since there really is a distinction to be marked between things we call solid and things we call liquid and gaseous, we kept talking about solidity in the same way but with the understanding that solidity is something different than we had thought. By contrast, film motion is not a paradigmatic case of motion. If we discovered that paradigmatic cases actually involve an object being stationary in 24 slightly different positions at 24 different moments in a second, then we might say that motion consists in something other than we thought and film images move paradigmatically. But when Currie asks us to acknowledge a new kind of response-dependent motion, he is not suggesting that we have been confused about the nature of ordinary motion all along.

This is the point at which Kania brings the debate to a close. He concludes that the initial objection to Currie's notion of real, response-dependent film motion remains: By invoking the category of response-dependent properties, Currie secures the reality of film motion only by destroying, or at least severely depleting, the category of illusions as a whole.

It is worth noting that the illusionist can allow for technical conditions under which the film image really would be moving. Kania asks us to imagine that the impression of motion is generated by a projector continuously shining light through a single film frame that changes over time – perhaps, as Kania suggests, the frame is a liquid crystal display controlled by a computer. Since the images projected on screen would parallel the actual movements within the frame, they would really be continuously and contiguously moving.[73] Kania sees no problem with saying that the same film projected in the standard way and projected in this special way really moves in the latter case but not in the former case. At the very least, the comparison between the two cases makes it more difficult to say that the standardly projected film really does move: 'Just as you can set up what looks like a Müller-Lyer illusion, but in which the line that looks longer *actually is* longer, there can be something that you might assume to be an illusion of movement but which is in fact an example of movement proper'.[74]

Carroll, on the other hand, would likely find such a position incoherent. In response to a different case, he insists that to say that the same film viewed in the cinema and viewed at home on the television really moves in the latter case and not in the former is 'patently contradictory'.[75] The mechanism that generates the impression of movement in the cinema – namely, the projector – can (at least in principle) be deconstructed in such a way that we can see with the naked eye how movement is generated. But the mechanism that generates the impression of movement on TV cannot be deconstructed in an analogous way. If the slowed-down projector is the test for an illusion of movement, and the same kind of test cannot be conducted on a TV-screening of a certain film, Carroll suggests that the illusionists' argument is defeated simply by the introduction of new technology for screening films.

This is rather a hasty conclusion, however. There could be other kinds of test applied to other kinds of film-screening technology that reveal perceived motion to be an illusion. Just because the slowed-down projector test fails to apply to films shown on TV, the illusionist is not forced to conclude that the motion on TV is real. To think otherwise is to set up a false dichotomy. And even if there are no such tests for the illusion of movement produced by other film-screening technologies, this need not affect the illusionists' argument for the case of films projected in the traditional way. While some illusionists might like to show that film motion is always an illusion, there is nothing contradictory about their saying that, depending on how the impression of motion is generated, it either is or is not illusory.

CONCLUSIONS

As a reminder, here is what we have covered in this chapter:

1. Bazin's confused but fascinating attempt to show that there is a single realist film style that realizes the true purpose of photographically-based film.
2. Walton's argument for the transparency of photographs that preserves the Bazinian insight that the realism of photographs derives from the photographic process.
3. The critical response to Walton that raises questions about the conditions for seeing through a photograph, the very possibility – given the nature of perception – of seeing through a photograph or any other kind of mediator, and potentially significant differences between seeing through photographs and seeing through other things such as mirrors and microscopes.
4. Currie's argument for the realism of depiction and the superior depictive potential of film media.
5. The debate between Currie, Carroll and Kania about whether the traditionally projected film image really moves just because we cannot help but see it move.

Before taking up the question of film motion, we had come full circle in our quest for a proper understanding of the pictorial realism of film.

Currie's critique of Walton's broadly Bazinian account of photographic transparency leads him to give an account of film realism that also preserves some of Bazin's central insights. Currie himself declares that one's view about the pictorial realism of film does not entail a particular view about the realism of motion in film.[76] But in true Bazinian spirit, Currie seems compelled to push realism as far as it will go in accounting for the nature of film. Perhaps you think he has gone too far when he posits a new kind of response-dependent motion. But if nothing else, Currie's view about film motion forces us to a new awareness of the grounds of the commonsense illusion view. Such an awareness is invaluable given the increasing diversification of technological means for generating the impression of motion in film.

CHAPTER 3

AUTHORSHIP

In Chapters 1 and 2, we learnt that photographically-based film has distinctive capacities for artistically significant effects like representation, expression, formal play and realism. We might, therefore, assume that someone who creatively exploits these capacities is a film artist. More generally, if there are works of film art, then surely there must be film artists. But who are they? Given the technically complex and frequently collaborative nature of filmmaking, it is often difficult to know where to assign creative ownership and responsibility. This problem is traditionally construed as a problem about the authorship of a film, which reflects the long-standing influence of the literary paradigm in film theory. In this chapter we will consider whether some films have authors and what role, if any, the film author plays in interpretation and criticism. We will encounter various complications along the way, most notably with the distinction between an actual author – an actual person with a crucial role in filmmaking, often thought to be the director, and an implied author – an imagined figure constructed in interpretation. But before we enter into the debate about film authorship, we need to gain a sense of its history.

The tradition of thinking about film in terms of authorship or creative individuality first gained prominence in France with the film journal that Bazin co-founded in 1951, the *Cahiers du Cinéma*. The critics of the *Cahiers* advocated a new approach to filmmaking which would result in '*auteur* cinema,' '*auteur*' just being the French word for 'author'. The critic spearheading the campaign for the new approach was François Truffaut, who later became an important New Wave director.

In the January 1954 edition of *Cahiers*, Truffaut mounted an attack on what he called the 'tradition of quality' in French filmmaking which involved the adaptation of French literary classics. Films in this tradition were, according to Truffaut, derivative, stuffy and stylistically formulaic. Most importantly, they failed to explore the possibilities of the film medium. In contrast, *auteur* film was inherently cinematic, bearing the mark of an original and creative '*cinéaste*'. Among French directors,

Truffaut points to Jean Renoir and Robert Bresson as making innovative and highly individual films. These directors were more easily able to do this because they wrote their own screenplays. But with vision and a proper appreciation of film form, even a director working with someone else's screenplay in a restrictive studio system could contribute to '*auteur* cinema'. Thus Truffaut and other *Cahiers* critics celebrated the work of many Hollywood directors, including Alfred Hitchcock, Orson Welles, Robert Aldrich and Nicholas Ray. Moreover, when the American critic, Andrew Sarris, tried to turn Truffaut's ideas into a theory of criticism, he went so far as to claim that *only* studio directors working with other people's screenplays are candidates for the highest *auteur* status.

The sudden popularity of American film among post-war French critics was partly due to historical circumstance. During the Liberation period in France, all the Hollywood films from the late 1930s and early 1940s that had been banned during the Occupation, flooded into Paris. The heady experience of watching so many American films closely together gave French *cinéphiles* a unique appreciation of continuities of style and the emerging personalities of directors across bodies of work. Thus in his 1957 *Cahiers* article, 'La Politique des *auteur*s,' Bazin described auteurist critical practice as 'choosing in the artistic creation the personal factor as a criterion of reference, and then postulating its permanence and even its progress from one work to the next'.[77]

The aims of the *Cahiers* critics who advocated *auteur* cinema were polemical rather than theoretical. Truffaut's aims, in particular, were to make room for a new kind of filmmaking in the conservative and hierarchical French system, and force an appreciation of distinctly cinematic achievements by individual artists. Unavoidably, however, Truffaut committed himself to various theoretical assumptions which were later articulated by Sarris. The problem, as we shall discover, was that once the theory behind auteurist practice was made explicit, its contradictions and limitations were hard to ignore.

Since Sarris thinks that a good film is typically the product of a good director, he works to specify directorial standards that also function as critical standards. Criticism of these standards coincided with a larger theoretical shift in film studies under the influence of semiotics and structuralism. At first, attempts were made to reconcile the role of the *auteur* with a new emphasis on the impersonal codes and structures that supposedly run across groups of films. *Auteur*-structuralism was one such attempt: Emerging in the late 1960s, it postulated the *auteur* as the structuring unconscious latent in the work of a particular director.

On this view, the actual director cannot be the *auteur* because the *auteur* is a function of a particular kind of film analysis. The immediate result of the structuralist influence was thus a shift from thinking of the *auteur* as an actual person – for example, the directors Renoir and Bresson, to thinking of the *auteur* as a critical construct. In literary theory, the move from structuralism to post-structuralism meant that that the author-figure came to be regarded with great suspicion. If you have read any post-structuralist or postmodern literary theory – particularly the work of Michele Foucault or Roland Barthes, you will already know about the ultimate rejection of the notion of authorship as a repressive principle of interpretation. This idea has had significant influence over film theory. And yet, film critics have continued to refer to the author or *auteur*, as though we cannot help but think of certain films as the product of a creative plan or as vehicles for personal expression.

Recently, philosophers have become interested in the tenacity of the notion of the film author. By formulating a clear conception of the film author and her role in interpretation and criticism, philosophers can hope to return some theoretical legitimacy to the enduring critical interest in authorship. But as we shall discover, this is no easy task, particularly because the authorship debate takes up three different kinds of claim about the film author. Most of the theorists we will consider touch upon all three. However, it is fair to say that traditional *auteur*ists like Sarris were mostly concerned with the third claim, *auteur*-structuralists were mostly concerned with the second claim, and contemporary philosophers are mostly concerned with the first claim:

1. The ontological claim: Many films are authored. A film can be seen as the creative product of a single individual.
2. The interpretive claim: The best way to understand a film is as the creative product of a single individual – that is, as manifesting an individual's artistic vision.
3. The evaluative claim: We can judge a film to be good or bad on the basis of its author's reputation or creative struggle.

In order to defend either the interpretive or the evaluative claim, one first has to assume the ontological claim. But there is a fundamental challenge to the ontological claim which derives from the way most films are made. If you are someone who likes to watch the credits roll at the end of a film screening, you will know just how many technicians, craftspeople and artists are involved in any given film project. Many of the roles listed in the credits – from lead actor to best boy, are highly specialized such that it is unlikely that any one person involved in the project – even the director or producer, controls every detail of the film-making process. And yet despite knowing how complex and collaborative filmmaking can be, we still regularly credit films to a single person, usually the director. Is this just a convenient shorthand or does it reflect some truth about film authorship? The question that a defender of the film author needs to confront is whether it makes sense to claim authorship for films that are serially manufactured – in other words, the vast majority of films, made by a series of specialists – from the screenwriter all the way to the editor, building on each other's work at each stage of production. There are several replies to the question of whether serially manufactured films can have authors:

1. The director can be the sole author of a film because his role in supervising and coordinating the activities of others determines the aesthetic significance of the film.
2. Someone (or something) besides the director can be sole author for the same reason that their role determines the aesthetic significance of the film – for example, the screenwriter, the star, the producer or even the studio system.
3. Insofar as there are multiple artistic collaborators on a film project, there can be multiple authors of a film.
4. A film can have a single, implied author who is constructed to help with understanding the film.
5. Films do not have authors. Their aesthetic significance is not determined by a generative agent, actual or implied. Instead, their aesthetic significance might be determined by unconscious forces or by the audience.

In this chapter, we will discover that there is some truth in every one of these replies.

WHO IS THE CINEMATIC AUTHOR?

To ask this question makes it sound as though a crucial assumption about the nature of authorship in film has already been made; namely, that there is only ever one author for an authored film. There could be several reasons why most theorists interested in authorship make this assumption.

For example, it could be due to the influence of the literary paradigm and its emphasis on single authorship, or the influence of the Romantic conception of artists as solitary, tortured souls aiming at personal expression. Whatever the reason, however, there is an important challenge to the single authorship assumption, which we will consider in the form of an argument by a contemporary philosopher, Berys Gaut. Before we do this, however, let us consider the most common answer to our starting question, which is that, if a film has an author at all, it is the director.

It is easy to understand why this answer is so popular. Among ordinary filmgoers, it is common practice to identify films by their directors – as, for example, when we talk about seeing the latest Scorcese or admiring the work of Ang Lee. It is also common practice for critics to refer to a certain kind of director as an *auteur*, one whose films are all recognizably hers. However, as well as the assumption of single authorship, claiming that a film's author is the director rests upon a second, crucial assumption; namely, that the cinematic author is a real person. As we know from our brief survey of the history of authorship in film studies, a shift away from thinking of the author as a real person and towards thinking of him as an interpretive construct occurred under the influence of semiotics and structuralism.

One reason to be wary about making the author a real person derives from the single authorship assumption. If one is hesitant to single out one of the many real-life collaborators on a film project as the film's author but nevertheless holds onto the assumption that a film can only have one author, then one may be attracted to the idea of constructing a single author for a suitably unified collaborative film. Other reasons for adopting a constructivist view of authorship are tied up with particular theoretical commitments. For example, we shall see that Peter Wollen's commitment to structuralist analysis leads him to identify the director's unconscious preoccupations, as they emerge throughout a body of work, with an implied author. As well, under the influence of postmodern literary theory, some film theorists conceive of authorship as one subject position among many in relation to 'reading' the film 'text'.

But maybe we have got ahead of ourselves. Before considering who occupies the authorial role in film, we must make sure that we understand what this role consists in. In other words, we must have a solid conception of the author, which fits both with the ordinary use of the term and its use in discourse about the arts. In what follows, we will compare two philosophical conceptions of the author: Paisley Livingston's realist conception and Alexander Nehamas's constructivist – or, as he likes to call it, transcendental – conception.

The most general definition of an author in the Oxford English Dictionary is 'the person who originates or gives existence to anything'. As well, however, an author can be an inventor, constructor or founder, the cause of events, a prompter or mover, an authority or informant, a composer or writer, a director, ruler or commander, and even the 'one who begets' – in other words, a father or ancestor. In discourse about the arts, the author is first and foremost the creator of a literary work. Architects and composers are sometimes referred to as authors, as well as the creative authority behind a large-scale artistic project like the ceiling of the Sistine Chapel. But the literary author is paradigmatic; indeed, even outside discourse about the arts, this kind of author may be the first that comes to mind for many people.

If we want to apply the literary notion of authorship to film, we need to decide how the literary notion is related to the complex ordinary-language notion. In the past, literary theorists with certain agendas have been tempted merely to stipulate a use of the term 'author'. But, as the contemporary philosopher, Paisley Livingston, points out with particular reference to Michel Foucault, a stipulated usage is not going to help us make sense of how we already think about the author. This leads Livingston to a pragmatic analysis of the term as a means of attribution for the sake of establishing socio-cultural context or the proper target of critique and response. The result is a 'provisional' definition of 'author' as a 'term of art' which coincides with but also helps disambiguate ordinary usage of the term. According to Livingston, an author is 'an agent who intentionally makes an utterance, where the making of an utterance is an action, an intended function of which is expression or communication'.[78]

For an action to be an utterance it must be intended to express or communicate some attitude, be it a desire, belief, or intention. The fact that we are in control of and responsible for our utterances is enough to make us authors of them, even if most of our utterances are trite, formulaic, or unimaginative. To be the author of a particular utterance of 'Good Morning', one need not have invented the phrase or the social function it fulfils. One says it on purpose, though not necessarily with deliberation, and in so doing, exercises 'one's linguistic and social know-how'.[79] Authorship on Livingston's account is therefore just a fact of our being rational, social, and discursive creatures; it is part of a 'pragmatic framework' that 'remains a deeply entrenched, valuable, and arguably indispensable schema of interaction. It is, moreover, a schema that we frequently apply in discussions of the arts'.[80]

Even though Livingston does not explore this possibility for the case of studio film, his definition allows for a single utterance having multiple authors – the example he gives is of John and Mary jointly sending a video letter to their parents with holiday greetings and news.[81] For John and Mary to be joint-authors requires that they both intend to express their own attitudes in the letter – for example, they are not being coerced into saying things they don't mean, and though each of them may not know exactly what the other will say during taping, they each know that the other is committed to the same, shared project.[82] This example also serves to highlight the fact that an utterance need not be linguistic. There are many different kinds of expressive and communicative actions, as well as products of these actions – a film, for example – that are authored because they are 'identified with reference to the relevant features of their context of production'.[83]

Whereas Livingston gives us an entirely general account of the actual author, which he himself later applies to film, Nehamas gives us a specifically literary account of the implied author, which it is up to us to apply to film. Despite their many differences, these accounts share an emphasis on action and intention. According to Nehamas, when we construct an author for a literary work, we are thinking of the work as the product of an action such that we make sense of it by conceiving of its possible motivation. The one who 'owns' the hypothesized action behind the work is the author. The sense in which one owns an action is very different from the sense in which one owns a pair of shoes or a car: One cannot be separated from one's actions, since an agent and her agency are mutually defined. This helps explain why Nehamas construes the author's ownership of the action resulting in a literary work in terms of the author being part of that work.

According to Nehamas, when we construe a text as a particular work, we create a context for that text that can be extended as far as interest allows. If you are trying to figure out why someone performed a certain action – say murdering his lover, you can stop at the immediate cause – say, the murderer's discovery of his lover's infidelity, or you can keep going and find other more distant causes. After all, murder is not the only way that one can respond to the discovery of infidelity. Why did the jealous lover commit murder instead of just shouting and throwing things or ending the relationship? In other words, why *this* particular action?

In order to answer this question, you are going to have to think harder about the jealous lover's other past experiences, general psychological tendencies and expectations. This involves expanding the explanatory context for his action. According to Nehamas, this is also what we do in interpretation, understood in terms of expansion rather than in terms of depth and hidden meaning. The one difference is that in interpretation, we cannot interrogate the agent whose action we are trying to understand. Instead we imagine what the agent would have to be like to have performed the particular action that results in the literary work.

Fortunately, our imagining can be guided by knowledge of the actual, historical figure who wrote the text that we are interpreting. Nehamas argues that the author can be considered 'a plausible historical variant of the writer, a character the writer could have been, someone who means what the writer could have meant, but never, in any sense, did mean'. A writer as an actual person cannot control and is not aware of all the features of her writing. 'But the author, produced jointly by writer and text, by work and critic, is not a person; it is a character who is everything the text shows it to be and who in turn determines what the text shows'.[84] We are not, therefore, going to conceive of a medieval text written by a medieval monk as having a modern author. We are going to think of the work in relation to other medieval works and construct an author with a suitably medieval motivation. But this process is open-ended in that we can keep comparing the work to other works and complicating the explanatory context for the author's activity.

We now have two very different conceptions of the author available to us – Livingston's pragmatic conception of the author as any actual person who performs an utterance, and Nehamas's transcendental conception of the author as a construct generated by and through literary interpretation. The next question to consider is whether we can apply either or both conceptions to film. In the following section, we will examine Livingston's use of a modified version of his conception to show that some serially manufactured films have single authors. Then we will consider the way that *auteur*-structuralist, Peter Wollen, constructs an author in his interpretation of groups of films by particular directors.

DO FILMS HAVE AUTHORS?

The obvious place to start in adapting Livingston's broad definition of authorship for film is by replacing 'utterance' with 'cinematic utterance'.

Livingston suggests that 'an utterance is a cinematic one just in case the agent or agents who produce it employ photographic (and other) means in order to create an apparently moving image projected on a screen (or other surface)'.[85]

Now the question is whether there are any serially manufactured films which count as the product of a cinematic utterance such that they count as authored. Livingston uses a series of real and imagined cases to show that, on his account, there are some serially manufactured films which clearly are not authored; there are others which are authored to a certain degree; and there are still others that are successfully completely authored. These cases ultimately reveal two criteria for full authorship: sufficient control over the final cut, since the final cut is the primary means by which a cinematic author can intend to make some attitudes manifest; and, having in mind some particular attitudes for the final cut to manifest. Thus the kind of control had by a film author involves having and being able to implement some kind of creative plan. Insofar as either the plan or its implementation can be partly compromised, a film can be only partly authored. Although this may frequently occur under studio conditions, full authorship remains a very real possibility – as Livingston demonstrates with the case of Ingmar Bergman's *Winter Light* (1962).

In the making of *Winter Light*, Bergman was crucially involved at every stage. He wrote his own script, did some of the casting, coached the actors, supervised the editing and sound-mixing, and worked closely with the cinematographer. He also exercised a high degree of control over the choice of location, props and make-up. Even those elements of the film that he did not help create himself – like the music by Bach – he appropriates for his own particular ends. At no point in production was Bergman coerced into changing his creative plan. To illustrate the balance achieved by Bergman between control and collaboration, Livingston compares him to the foreman of a construction project. Just as a foreman discusses the building plan with his crew and then trusts them to carry out specific tasks under his direction, so Bergman aims to share his artistic vision with his collaborators in order to constrain and synchronize their specialized roles.[86]

In claiming sole authorship for Bergman, Livingston is not overlooking the fact that many other talented people worked on *Winter Light*. His point is just that all the other collaborators were working to make *Bergman's* film, to realize *Bergman's* artistic vision. In other words, being an artistic contributor to a project does not make one its co-author unless one 'exercises decisive control over the creative process and takes credit for the work'.[87] This distinction between a non-controlling artistic contributor and an author is not one that everyone recognizes, however. Gaut, in particular, considers anyone who makes 'a significant artistic difference to the work' to have a share in its ownership. In painting, for example, it is now standard to ascribe a work, not just to a master painter like Rembrandt, but also to the master's workshop. But even though there is collaboration in many of the arts, Gaut goes on to note that the artistic effects of collaboration in film tend to be far more significant.[88]

Compare the case of film with that of architecture: When we say that a building is *by* Frank Gehry, we mean that Gehry is its sole author even though he has no hand in its actual construction. The builders are not Gehry's co-authors because their work involves simply realizing Gehry's design. Whereas Gehry can specify the exact dimensions of his building and the exact materials to be used in its construction, a film director has to leave it up to her collaborators to decide exactly how to carry out many of their assigned tasks. There are simply too many possible dimensions of variation in how these tasks are performed; practically speaking, a single person could not issue directorial instructions precise enough to accommodate every possible variation. The task of acting illustrates this point nicely: No amount of directorial instruction can control exactly how an actor says his lines and the exact nuances of emotion and meaning that he brings to them. The director cannot simply manipulate actors like puppets in order to realize her personal artistic vision through them, and yet an actor's performance may contribute significantly to the aesthetic significance of a film – take for example, Daniel Day Lewis's magnificent performance in *There Will be Blood* (2008). This suggests to Gaut that at least some film actors are co-authors alongside the director. [89]

The same is not true for theatre actors, however. Gaut points to a fundamental ontological difference between film, as an audio–visual recording art, and theatre, as a literary art, that explains why theatre actors are not usually co-authors of the plays which they perform. Since a play is individuated by its script, the playwright fully determines the characters before they are portrayed by different actors. No doubt the first portrayal of Othello by the famous Renaissance actor, Richard Burbage, was very different from the acclaimed early-twentieth century portrayal by Paul Robeson. But the fact remains that both Burbage and Robeson are portraying the same character from Shakespeare's play. By contrast, a character in a film cannot be fully determined by, say, a screenwriter or a director before he is portrayed by an actor on camera.

This is because a recorded performance is part of what makes a film what it is; namely a series of moving images, (often) with sound. Since a film cannot be performed but instead incorporates recorded performances, and since film actors give the performances that, when recorded, become part of the film as an object of aesthetic appreciation, Gaut argues that actors are one kind of film collaborator among many that have a claim to authorship.

Whereas Gaut is willing to count as a film's author anyone who plays an aesthetically significant role in its production, Livingston only counts as a film's author someone for whom the film is a direct and personal vehicle of expression. This means that, overall, Gaut will consider many more serially manufactured films than Livingston to be authored. But he will consider far fewer films than Livingston to have actual, single authors.

In the case of large-scale studio film production, if not in the case of small-scale independent, amateur, or experimental film production, one might be tempted to give up trying to identify an actual, single author for a film and instead settle for constructing an author when it helps with interpretation. But can we do this? Can we intelligibly and usefully construct a single author for a highly collaborative film in the way that Nehamas suggests we construct a single author for a literary work? In order to answer this question, we will first assess one form that the constructivist strategy has taken in film theory. Then we will consider some general objections to the constructivist strategy.

In the late 1960s, a group of British film theorists under the influence of the French structural anthropologist, Claude Lévi-Strauss, developed a new approach to film interpretation called *auteur*-structuralism. On this approach, the *auteur* is both the product and locus of structural analysis. On Lévi-Strauss's model, structural analysis involves tracing the complex cultural expression of various binary opposites that structure our thinking. Applying this model to film, *auteur*-structuralists tried to identify the basic binary motifs that characterize a body of work and trace the development of their expression. The way that the *auteur* enters into this approach is by representing the source of the structure of thinking expressed in the structure of a certain group of films. According to one leading *auteur*-structuralist, Peter Wollen, the *auteur* is identified with the 'film unconscious' or its expression in the binary thematic structure of the film. Thus the basic oppositions between garden and wilderness, and nature and culture that characterize films by John Ford are attributed to 'Ford' the *auteur*, the imagined mind, but not to the actual person,

Ford, since his relationship to the film is mediated by the work of other collaborators.[90]

According to Wollen, the *auteur*-structuralist approach reinforces many of our common judgments about the work of different directors. The richness and complexity of Ford's films at the level of structural analysis explains their widely recognized critical importance. In turn, this suggests that the value of a film like *The Searchers* (1956) lies in its potential for re-structuring culture and our thinking. Thus Wollen concludes, '[a] valuable work, a powerful work at least, is one which challenges codes, overthrows established ways of reading or looking, not simply to establish new ones, but to compel an unending dialogue, not at random but productively'.[91]

We will return to the question of what makes a film good or bad for an *auteur*ist in the next section (and we will examine the nature of so-called cinematic 'codes' in the next chapter). First we need to consider whether the general strategy behind *auteur*-structuralism – the strategy of constructing an *auteur* as part of film interpretation – is a good one. The reason we will evaluate this general strategy and not the specifics of *auteur*-structuralism is because, in the history of film theory, *auteur*-structuralism represents little more than a temporary bridge between two opposed methodologies. As the film author was swept away by the tide of postmodernism, *auteur*-structuralism was abandoned before it was fully developed.

Let us, therefore, return to a more general question: Can we really construct a film author? Nehamas suggests that to do so in literary interpretation is an inevitable result of construing a text as a work – the product of an imagined action. But what of film interpretation? Is it also the case that we can make sense of a film in terms of an imagined filmmaker with a particular motivation? Once again, this brings us back to the complex and highly collaborative nature of filmmaking. Even if you do not know much about filmmaking, the film itself, with its diverse combination of visual and acoustic elements, betrays something of the enormity of the task of its creation. But if one has this sense of a film's collaborative origins, perhaps it would be difficult and unhelpful to attribute the final work to a single, imagined author. We would have to imaginatively ascribe to this author responsibility for every aspect of a film from its musical score to its lighting and cinematography, and even all the performances of the actors. But then, as Gaut suggests, we would be working with such an alien entity, one with superhuman abilities such as the ability to control actors like puppets while simultaneously planning every camera move, that we would not be able to understand the author's motivation. According to Nehamas, the whole point of constructing an author is to rationalize a work as the product of a particular action, ascribable to a particular kind of agent with a particular motivation.

The difficulty in fully imagining a single, implied author for a serially manufactured film could explain the vagueness of Wollen's description of the *auteur* as 'an unconscious catalyst' after whom the defining structure of a group of films is named. Indeed, it is difficult to see why Wollen bothers with the *auteur* at all if he is really interested in structures and codes. In Gaut's case, however, he remains sensitive to the way that film interpretation is guided by signs of creative intelligence in the work itself. But he insists that these signs do not need to be signs of a single author; they can be signs of multiple authors who we may imagine as coordinating their creative activities more or less successfully in a more or less unified film.

Even if it is difficult, in the case of studio film, to imagine a single author, the method of interpretation involving the construction of authors is still permitted by Gaut. Livingston, on the other hand, sees little to recommend such a method: Either a film has an actual author, in which case there is no need to construct one, or it does not have an actual author, and then it would be misleading to imagine that it does.

AUTHOR-BASED FILM CRITICISM

Thus Livingston, unlike the constructivists, does not view the attribution of authorship as an integral and essential part of film interpretation. We can only decide on a case-by-case basis whether a film's expressed attitudes can be seen as the intended results of an actual author's activities. Of course this requires us to know quite a bit about how a film was made and many ordinary viewers do not seek out this kind of information before watching a film. But Livingston insists that this does not make such information any less valuable for interpretation. Any interpretation that we offer of a film has to match up with relevant features of that film, and some of those features will be tied to the film's 'causal history'.[92] However, Livingston would be the first to admit that only for certain films will these causal features be features of authorship. He does not specify the differences in how we interpret films with and without authors. And although his example of Bergman's *Winter Light* suggests a connection between the value of a film and its having a visionary author, Livingston does not develop a theory of author-based criticism. By contrast, for traditional *auteur*ists, this was precisely the goal behind the first step of identifying a film's actual author.

The idea developed by the critics of the *Cahiers*, particularly François Truffaut, that there is a certain kind of film-maker who makes truly cinematic and personally expressive films, was imported to the United States in the early 1960s by the film critic, Andrew Sarris. Keeping '*auteur*' as the label for this kind of director, Sarris formulated explicit principles for author-based film criticism. These were to be applied to American film, which ever since the First World War had been almost entirely based in Hollywood. Tired of the critical overshadowing of Hollywood 'entertainment' by European 'art' film, Sarris saw *auteur* theory as a way of elevating the American director and celebrating the rich tradition of American film. As a more 'scholarly' approach compared to the 'subjective perils of impressionistic and ideological' journalistic criticism, Sarris also saw *auteur* theory as a way to institutionalize the study of film in North America.[93] While acknowledging the established European and Asian *auteurs*, Sarris recasts the American director as a cowboy-figure engaged in a heroic creative struggle against the oppressive machinery of the Hollywood studio system. Notable 'cowboys' include Raoul Walsh, Howard Hawks, and John Ford. The good director, according to Sarris, makes good films by winning his struggle against the system. The critic's task is to identify the signs of a successful struggle across a director's body of work.

In particular, the critic looks for three things: Signs of technical competence on the part of the director, signs of the director's personality, and signs of the creation of what Sarris calls, 'interior meaning'. Since a Hollywood director is usually working with someone else's script, his personality emerges, not in the subject-matter of his films, but in his treatment of the material. The inevitable tension that persists between a film's material and directorial personality is the source of interior meaning. Although interior meaning is supposed to be the highest mark of a film's value, Sarris admits that it is hard to say what it is exactly. This is because interior meaning 'is imbedded in the stuff of the cinema and cannot be rendered in noncinematic terms'. The most we can do is point to examples of moments in particular films when we are brought to recognize interior meaning. The example Sarris gives is, surprisingly, not from an American film: It is a particular scene in *Rules of the Game* (1939) when the character Octave (played by the director, Jean Renoir) pauses in his 'bearishly shambling journey to the heroine's boudoir'.

Sarris remarks, '[i]f I could describe the musical grace note of that momentary suspension, and I can't, I might be able to provide a more precise definition of the *auteur* theory'.[94]

The more closely you study a body of work, comparing films by the same director, the more instances of the expression of personality and interior meaning you will find. In other words, you will notice greater stylistic continuity across a body of work – say, through the repeated use of a particular narrative device, and you will gain a stronger sense of the director's particular outlook and sensibility. The 'joys of the *auteur* theory' derive from the surprising discoveries the critic can make in her comparative analysis. Ultimately, then, Sarris seems to recommend his critical approach as a way to get more out of watching studio films. But whether the approach has internal coherence and intuitive plausibility is a further question.

It is another American critic, and one of Sarris's contemporaries, who pursues this question most vehemently. Pauline Kael makes no effort to hide her derision for *auteur* theory, and sometimes sacrifices logical argument for the sake of witty retort. Nevertheless, she raises some important objections to Sarris's evaluative criteria.[95] Technical competence, Kael argues, cannot be a prerequisite for good direction because there are directors whose greatness derives in part from their inventiveness in the absence of technical competence – her example is the Italian director, Michelangelo Antonioni. As for the expression of personality in the treatment of material, this is not just unnecessary for a good film, but might actually make for a bad film. This is because we tend to notice the personality of the director most in his worst films, those that simply re-use particularly effective devices that characterize his style. By linking uniformity of style and the expression of personality, *auteur* theory ends up celebrating, not artistic originality, but the mastery of a set of 'tricks' for manipulating the audience. The result is that 'often the works *auteur* critics call masterpieces are ones that seem to reveal the contempt of the director for the audience'.[96]

Finally, Kael considers interior meaning, the ultimate stamp of the *auteur*, and decides that it is illusory. For one thing, it is rare to find the kind of tension that is supposed to be productive of interior meaning because any 'competent commercial director generally does the best he can with what he's got to work with'. But even if there is such tension in a film, Kael asks, 'what kind of meaning could you draw out of it except that the director's having a bad time with lousy material or material he doesn't like?'.[97] Looking for interior meaning is just the *auteur* critics' excuse for repeatedly watching mediocre films, films which only display the requisite tension at the expense of a unity of form and content.

Much of the force of Kael's attack on Sarris derives from her conviction that *auteur* theory violates the ethics of criticism. It does this, she thinks, by encouraging praise for the occasional bad film by a favoured director and censure of the occasional good film by an unpredictable director, as well as by regarding any director who works with her own material as suspect. Thus despite the vitriol, Kael's analysis reminds us of the danger that author-based criticism become merely a cult of personality. From what we have seen in this chapter, this danger might be avoided in at least two ways: By referring to a single, implied author instead of the actual director, or by acknowledging the authorial role of multiple collaborators. This is not to deny, however, that a suitably qualified reference to the director of a film could also guide interpretation and appreciation.

CONCLUSIONS

Author-based criticism is of course not the only form of film evaluation. In Chapter 5, we will consider other forms that involve only peripheral reference to the film-maker. The point of considering author-based criticism here is that it involves certain assumptions about the nature and status of the film author. Despite disagreement over the acceptability of these assumptions, participants in the film authorship debate can agree that in the complex and highly collaborative production of serially manufactured films, there is often a dominant collaborator and this is often the director. It would be interesting to try to articulate what it is about the role of a director and film culture in general that often makes the director assume dominance in the minds of critics and ordinary viewers. But the more pressing philosophical question concerns whether a dominant collaborator has creative ownership over a film, and if so, what kind. As we have learnt, there are several ways of answering this question: The dominant collaborator on a particular film could be

1. the sole author;
2. one author among many; or
3. not an author at all.

If we choose the third answer, this could be for one of two reasons:

i. with a multitude of collaborators, there can be no actual authors; or
ii. the author is not an actual person but an interpretive construct.

Finally, even if we accept that the dominant collaborator on a particular film is its actual author, we can still interpret the film in terms of the role of an implied author.

These are the options for assigning authorship made available by our discussion in this chapter. There are, however, further considerations concerning new technology that might complicate these options. One such consideration derives from the introduction of DVDs.

As well as the film itself, many DVDs include commentary by directors and other collaborators, as well as out-takes and even alternate endings. A DVD may also give two or more versions of the same film. For example, in 2006, a two-DVD 'collector's edition' of *Apocalypse Now* (1979) was released, which includes both the original theatrical version of the film as well as the 2001 re-released version, *Apocalypse Now Redux*, with over 49 minutes of extra footage. The DVD set also includes such items as a clip of Marlon Brando reading T. S. Eliot's 'The Hollow Men', new production 'featurettes', and cast member interviews. It is interesting to consider whether the addition of all this 'supplementary material' makes it easier or more difficult to assign authorship.

On the one hand, the supplementary material may help us to determine whether the director's or some other collaborator's artistic aims have been realized in the final work. On the other hand, it may also draw our attention to the high degree of contingency and circumstance governing how this film, like any other massive production, turns out. In comparing the two versions of *Apocalypse Now* we could decide that one has an (actual or implied) author and the other does not, or that they have different (actual or implied) authors (which then raises the question of whether the two versions really count as two versions of the same film). One thing is clear, however. We would not be in a position to make any kind of decision about a complex case like *Apocalypse Now* on DVD without the work we have already done in this chapter – without first having carefully distinguished kinds of authorship, criteria for the assignment of authorship and criteria for author-based film criticism.

CHAPTER 4

THE LANGUAGE OF FILM

The influence of a literary paradigm is felt, not only in the debate about film authorship, but also in another debate that bridges classical and psycho-semiotic film theory. This is the debate about whether there is a language of film and, consequently, whether we understand and appreciate a film in fundamentally the same way as we understand and appreciate a literary work. Given that languages have to be learnt by grasping the conventions that govern the meaning of words and the operations of grammar, the possibility that film functions like a language has serious implications for its claim to realism. As we learnt in Chapter 2, the realism of film is often explained in terms of our seemingly natural ability to recognize on the film screen what was filmed. But if we are 'reading' film like a language, then this recognitional capacity is not natural, after all, but conventional, and the accessibility of film images cannot be taken as a sign of their realism. If we wish, therefore, to settle on a coherent picture of the nature of film, particularly in its traditional medium, we must take up the debate about film and language.

In the heyday of psycho-semiotic film theory, it was quite common for scholars to talk about the 'grammar' of the film or the shot,[98] and even today, it is common for scholars to talk about 'reading' a film or film genre.[99] In most of these instances, however, language terms are only being used metaphorically, and without any ontological commitments, to refer to different modes of film analysis and interpretation. This reflects a broader tendency in the arts to use language terms to suggest the seriousness and rigor of a particular mode of analysis or the elevated status of a certain art form or genre – as when art historians identify a mature style of painting or architecture in terms of its distinctive 'grammar'. But in relation to art in general, language terms are not only used metaphorically. Nelson Goodman, for example, does not call his seminal work in aesthetics, *Languages of Art*,[100] just because it sounds serious and intriguing. Rather, he uses this title because his work contains a theory about the language-like conventionality of artistic representation. Similarly, when film theorist Christian Metz uses language terms, it is not merely for rhetorical flourish. In his case, it is because he is applying the general semiotics of the Swiss linguist Ferdinand de Saussure to film. Since Saussure prioritized language as the paradigmatic semiotic system, it is not surprising that Metz refers to 'cinematographic language,' and aims 'to study the orderings and functionings of the main signifying units used in the cinematic message'.[101]

When language terms are used literally in relation to film, the philosopher naturally pricks her ears. Now we have a genuinely philosophical question to consider concerning the nature of film. The question of whether there is a language of film is not the question of whether films involve language – say with dialogue or text, but whether there is a language of film images. The images in a film are the individual shots, traditionally animated as a succession of frames passing before the projector beam, and then combined into sequences through editing. Thus the question of whether there is a language of film images is the question of whether individual shots and their combinations constitute a language. In other words, it is either the question of whether individual shots function like words or sentences, or it is the question of whether the combination of individual shots occurs in the same way as the combination of words and sentences. Furthermore, the question of whether shots function as words or sentences concerns whether they acquire their literal or intrinsic meaning in the same way as words and sentences. This means that the starting question, whether there is a language of film, tends to reduce to the question of whether we understand film as a language. When the focus is on narrative film, this question becomes even more focused: Do we understand the story in a film in the same way that we understand a story in a novel, say, which is written out in a familiar language?

Even though there may be no definition of language, we can agree on a range of uncontroversial examples like English, French and Arabic. These and other natural languages are the subject of linguistics, and the aim for many film theorists in defending the language-like nature of film is to qualify film for the rigours of linguistic analysis. Metz sums up this aim when he suggests that the precise, analytical methods of linguistics 'provide the semiotics of the cinema with a constant and precious aid in establishing units that, though they are still approximate, are liable over time (and, one hopes, through the work of many scholars) to become progressively refined'.[102] Given that the purpose of the film-language analogy is to qualify film for linguistic analysis, the best way to test the analogy is by comparing film to a language like English that already qualifies for such analysis.

In an initial comparison, we immediately see that the 'language' of film images is more limited than English in its modes of transmission and representation. Whereas English is available through all our senses – through sight in its written form, through hearing in its spoken form, through touch in Braille, and at least in principle through taste and smell in coded forms, film 'language' is only available to us through sight. Furthermore, in the written form of English, the wide variety of fonts and styles of handwriting suggest a degree of flexibility in exactly how we represent a natural language. But with a film image, there is no such flexibility: Any modification to how the image looks changes its meaning.[103] These differences raise interesting questions about whether film 'language' can be translated in the way that all natural languages can be translated into one another (albeit with some loss in shades of meaning). The Russian silent-film-maker and theorist, Vsevolod Pudovkin, argued that the task of the film director is to translate a fully written-out scenario, word-by-word, into images that are then edited together just as the words of the scenario are combined into sentences and phrases.[104] This might strike one as a highly idiosyncratic view of film-making, however. If it does, the underlying reason may have to do with further differences between language and film that we shall discuss in this chapter.

If you are already suspicious of the film-language analogy, you may want to consider a weaker claim: Not that film is a language, but that film belongs to a larger category which also includes languages. This is the category of semiotic systems or systems of signs. Other things that have been called semiotic systems include the natural languages, traffic signs, ships' signalling systems, the gestures of Trappist monks, semaphore, conventions of dress or costume, and even myths. Semiotics is the study of systems of signs and specifically the codes that determine the meaning of signs. Film semiotics, in particular, reduces the task of the film theorist and critic to one of 'de-coding' films, thereby determining, not just what every shot and sequence means, but how every shot and sequence means what it means – by what cultural, artistic or cinematic convention.

The questions whether film is a system of signs to be de-coded and whether film is a language are intertwined in psycho-semiotic film theory. Nevertheless, there are several concerns specific to the first question that we shall consider. These have to do with the implications of using key terms like 'code' and 'sign' in equivocal and ambiguous ways, as well as with the prospects for substantial theoretical results in the mere classification of conventions. Ultimately, however, our goal in this chapter is to see whether our understanding of the nature and value of film art is deepened or merely obfuscated by the comparison to language and other sign-systems.

FILM, LANGUAGE AND MONTAGE

Even though the film-language analogy is most fully developed in psycho-semiotic film theory, it is first made much earlier, during the era of silent film, by those Soviet film-makers and theorists, particularly Pudovkin and Sergei Eisenstein, who take editing or montage to be the defining feature of film art. Both Pudovkin and Eisenstein are interested in how the meaning of a film *qua* work of art, and not just the depictive meaning of its individual shots, is created in context through the process of montage. In order to emphasize the importance of montage for creating meaning and artistic value, Pudovkin makes a comparison between film and literature. In a literary work, he suggests, it is not the literal meaning of individual words that matters aesthetically but instead how the writer combines those words to create rich images and associations. The example Pudovkin uses involves the initial selection of the word, 'beech,' which, on its own, 'is only the raw skeleton of a meaning, so to speak, a concept without essence or precision'. When this word is combined in a phrase like, '"the tender green of a young beech,"' it is no longer 'merely a bare suggestion'. Rather, it 'has become part of a definite, literary form. The dead word has been waked to life through art'.[105] Pudovkin goes on to suggest that the individual words of a literary work are equivalent to the individual shots of a film. Thus in the same way, what those shots literally mean in terms of what they show is not aesthetically relevant, and the accumulated literal meaning of the shots is not equivalent to the meaning of the film. Rather, the creative combination of shots through editing yields the only meaning that matters for evaluating and interpreting a film.

One problem with this account is that in both the case of literature and the case of film, even though context is important for interpretation, literal meaning still matters. Thus to use Pudovkin's own example, it matters what the word 'beech' literally means in the phrase, 'the tender green of a young beech', even though it is only the phrase as a whole that gives us an image of this particular beech tree. It would make a difference to the connotative meaning of the line if, for example, the poet had written 'willow' or 'bicycle' instead of 'beech'. This problem reflects the limitations of the exclusive emphasis on editing among Soviet film-makers. Whereas it is undoubtedly true that editing adds meaning and value to a film, it is also true that a well-composed and expressive shot can have the same kind of meaning and value.

Another problem with Pudovkin's account is that words and shots resist comparison. As Metz will later point out, even a close-up shot of a single object – say a revolver – cannot be translated as the single word, 'revolver', 'but at the very least, and without speaking of the connotations, it signifies "Here is a revolver!"'.[106] Metz goes on to suggest that the shot is not even equivalent to a sentence, since it contains 'a quantity of undefined information'. All the detail contained in a shot of a landscape, say, could be expressed in a multitude of ways, in a multitude of sentences. Thus, Metz concludes, a shot is only equivalent to 'the complex statement of undefined length'.[107] This is also because a shot, like a statement and unlike a sentence, is always asserted – as indicated by Metz's translation of the close-up shot of a revolver as *'Here is* a revolver'. At this point one might be tempted to give up on the analogy between the shot and any part of language. We will return to this possibility a little further ahead. For now, it is enough to note that the word-shot analogy on which Pudovkin relies is problematic.

Like Pudovkin, Eisenstein is interested in the way that editing creates connotative meaning. But he seeks to avoid some of Pudovkin's difficulties by using a different language analogy: Instead of comparing film with literature, Eisenstein compares film, and specifically shot combinations, with a kind of character in Japanese writing, derived from Chinese writing, that he calls an ideogram. This kind of character refers to an abstract idea by means of combining and modifying pictographic characters that depict, in a stylized way, non-abstract objects associated with the idea. The Chinese character for 'bright', for example, combines the pictograms that represent the sun and the moon, and the Chinese character for 'good' combines the pictograms that represent a woman and a child. As Eisenstein describes the way such characters function, '[b]y the combination of two "depictables" is achieved the representation of something that is graphically undepictable'. Then he claims that this exact same process occurs in film. In virtue of editing, shots 'that are *depictive*, single in meaning, neutral in content' are combined 'into *intellectual* contexts and series'.[108]

Eisenstein's own films were the testing ground for his theory of 'intellectual montage'. In *October: Ten Days that Shook the World* (1927), a commemorative dramatization of the Bolshevik Revolution of October 1917, there is a famous sequence that juxtaposes a Baroque image of Jesus with images of Hindu deities, the Buddha, Aztec gods, and finally a primitive idol, in order to suggest the sameness of all religions. The idol is then compared with military regalia to suggest the linking of patriotism and religious fervour. In another sequence, shots of Alexander Kerensky, head of the pre-revolutionary Provisional Government, are interspersed with shots of a preening mechanical peacock, to suggest, quite clearly, the leader's vanity and decadence.

The fact that these shot sequences are so distinctive immediately raises doubts about the utility of Eisenstein's theory as a general account of the meaning of a film. Sometimes – perhaps most of the time, there is no conceptual meaning generated by a certain combination of images. When a fight scene in a Kung Fu movie is edited so that we see only the most salient moments of action, the meaning of the sequence depends upon the literal meaning of the individual shots, each depicting part of the action. In other words, the ordering of shots may not have any meaning beyond the meaning that it has for the action. Moreover, this case is not unusual, since we are often meant to pay attention, first and foremost, to what is shown, rather than what is merely suggested, on screen.

FILM SEMIOTICS

Motivated by a commitment to Bazinian realism, the next generation of theorists interested in film language are highly critical of Eisenstein's account. Metz, in particular, seems to think that the montagists over-emphasized symbolic meaning in film at the expense of depictive meaning. As a result, they failed to recognize the natural tendency of the film medium towards narrative – just by joining meaningful images together, a film tells a story. Thus according to Metz, '[g]oing from one image to two images, is to go from image to language'.[109]

Christian Metz has been called the most important film theorist since Bazin. Indeed, Alfred Guzzetti characterizes Metz's importance in terms of a dialogue between Metz and Bazin: With the title of his main work of film theory, Bazin asks, What is Cinema?, and Metz replies, 'cinema is a language'. Even if Metz is not the first film theorist to think of film in terms of language, Guzzetti insists that Metz is the first theorist to inform this way of thinking with a sophisticated understanding of linguistics, particularly the linguistics of Saussure.[110]

In fact, however, Metz's answer to Bazin's question is not so simple, precisely because he was working within the technical framework of Saussurian linguistics. On Metz's account, film is not just a language but a language without a system. This qualification reflects Saussure's distinction between *langue* and *parole*, or language and language system. *Langue* is the system of rules and conventions or codes that make up a language, independently of its use on particular occasions. *Parole* is an instance of language use. Saussure was most interested in *langue*, or the language system, and he might have said that every individual film is the *parole* of an underlying film *langue*. But Metz, based on his close study of film, argues that there is no underlying system of which individual films represent particular applications. There is just the film language being created as it is used in every film.

The language analogy holds for Metz insofar as film is fundamentally communicative – each film has a message for its viewers. But the analogy only goes so far because a film's message is available to us directly and naturally, and not by means of convention, given our ability to recognize what an image depicts. At some points in Metz's account, this seems to mean that the message of a particular film is not heavily coded. But Metz retreats from this claim in suggesting that the standard combination and organization of the natural signs of film images, particularly in the creation of a narrative, creates a cinematic code that it is the task of film semioticians[111] to analyse.

Metz is most interested in codes that are specific to the film medium, which include conventions of film punctuation like the fade in and out, and the dissolve, as well as conventions of montage for presenting the depictive material. According to Metz, a film is made up of basic units of meaning that he calls 'syntagmas'. In his analysis of narrative film, Metz arrives at a taxonomy of eight different kinds of syntagma. A series of shots that alternate between two events might constitute an 'alternate syntagma' insofar as it shows two events occurring simultaneously. Moreover, a series of shots showing a landscape might constitute a 'descriptive syntagma' insofar as it shows what the landscape is like rather than events unfolding over time. The reason that the syntagmas constitute codes is that they determine meaning conventionally, according to standard practices of montage. Thus, for example, even if the depicted content of individual shots in an alternating sequence is naturally available to us, we have to learn that the alternating sequence itself indicates simultaneity.

Metz assumes that the codes of film punctuation and montage concern denotation in film, or what the images in a film literally show us. But there are also codes that govern connotation in film, or the symbolic and expressive meaning that a shot or a series of shots acquires. For example, an American Gangster film might give an impression of foreboding in the way that it presents a scene of deserted wharves. While it is important to figure out the conventions governing the creation of such an impression, Metz gives priority to figuring out conventions governing denotation. In fact, however, it is not clear that Metz's distinction between denotation and connotation in a film can be upheld, since, as Gilbert Harman suggests, we figure out the plot of a film by referring both to what is shown and the way it is shown in context.[112] But even if the distinction could be upheld, another film semiotician, Peter Wollen, argues that Metz has his priorities wrong. It is connotative meaning and not denotative meaning that is the proper subject of film aesthetics and criticism. More generally, Wollen argues that Metz's analysis of cinematic codes and meaning is limited by Metz's adherence to the language analogy. For Wollen, since language is simply one kind of sign system among many, we must analyse film, not in terms of language, but just as another sign system.

For this kind of analysis, Wollen relies on a theory of signs given by the philosopher Charles Pierce who, along with Saussure, is considered to be a co-founder of semiotics. According to Pierce, a sign can function in three ways – as an icon, as an index, and as a symbol. According to Wollen, the film image can combine all three aspects of the sign. Insofar as a film image resembles its subject, it functions as an icon; insofar as a film image is causally related to its subject, it functions as an index; and, insofar as a film image bears connotative meaning as a result of context and convention, it functions as a symbol. A great film-maker is someone who can manipulate all three aspects of the sign, so that his films have 'pictorial beauty' (due to the iconic function), 'documentary truth' (due to the indexical function), and 'conceptual meaning' (due to the symbolic function). Wollen cites French New Wave director, Jean-Luc Godard, as an example of a film-maker who is great in this respect.[113]

By appealing to a general theory of signs, Wollen moves away from the linguistic analogy. Part of the reason that he is not tied to this analogy in the same way as Metz is that Wollen does not assume that film is essentially communicative and that every film carries a message. As works of art, films explore the implications of signs rather than simply using them to communicate. However, there are still codes for the film semiotician to study, which are the means by which we interpret the signs making up a film. According to Wollen, works of art 'exploit and call attention to various codes. The greatest works "interrogate" their own codes by pitting them against each other'.[114]

Despite their differences, then, Metz and Wollen agree that film theory and criticism is largely concerned with identifying, organizing and deciphering cinematic codes. But what, exactly, *is* a cinematic code? In ordinary language use, 'code' can mean either a cipher – in the sense of de-coding a message, or a convention or style – in the sense of codes of dress and military behaviour. The difficulty, according to Harman, is that film semioticians fail to mark this distinction in their use of the term. Thus, it is unclear whether Metz's syntagma taxonomy is an exercise in de-coding in the sense of explicating how a film has a meaning or in the sense of identifying structural features of a film. Similarly, when Wollen refers to the importance of iconography in film, and the codes of symbolic meaning on which it depends, he seems to be talking about style, expression, thematic material, and symbolism all at the same time. This leads Harman to accuse film semioticians of 'cheating' with their broad and loose use of the term 'code'. This usage, he argues, 'disguises the fact that much of aesthetics and criticism is properly concerned with something other than the significance of signs'.[115]

Remember, as well, that the ultimate purpose of both the language analogy and broader semiotic analysis in film theory is to help us account for the way that films acquire meaning, particularly story meaning, and thus how we understand them. But it is not clear that the work of film semioticians so far has contributed to an account of film interpretation. Take, once again, Metz's syntagma taxonomy: It may be satisfying to be able to identify and label the various standard relationships between edited shots. But being able to identify *when* I understand an alternating sequence as indicating simultaneity hardly explains *why* I understand the sequence in this way or what significance this has for my understanding of the story or film as a whole. And, in general, taxonomies of cinematic codes do not substitute for a theory of meaning or close contextual analysis of a particular film's narrative and narration.

LET'S FACE IT: FILM IS *NOT* A LANGUAGE!

These concerns about the efficacy and breadth of semiotic and language-based theoretical approaches to film are shared by the philosopher

Gregory Currie. His interest in understanding how language works in terms of communication leads him to confirm many of Metz's own worries about the weakness of the analogy between language and film. Ultimately, in showing just how different film is from language, Currie quashes Metz's hope of using linguistics to understand film. Currie goes further, however, to claim that, even if film could be compared to a language, this would not provide a method for interpreting the story of a film. This is because, in order to figure out what particular images mean for the story, we have to pay attention to context, or how the images fit with other images as well as with dialogue and other sound cues.

In setting up a comparison between film and language, Currie focuses on five features of a natural language like English that are 'salient in terms of communication,' and the logical relations between these features. English is both (1) productive and (2) conventional, and as a result, it is (3) recursive, (4) molecular and (5) acontextual. As we shall learn, film is also productive and many film language advocates have insisted on its conventionality. But film is not recursive, molecular and acontextual. Since these three features simply follow from the combination of productivity and conventionality, the fact that film does not have them is a decisive indicator of just how different film must be from language.

English is productive because an unlimited number of English sentences can be uttered and understood. We can use and understand sentences we have never heard before or that have never even been used before. As well, English is conventional because the meaning of its words and sentences is determined by how we use its words and sentences in certain standard ways in order to communicate with each other. Whereas, in principle, any word could have been used to designate the animal that we call a horse, we all stick to calling this animal a horse so that we can understand one another. As a result of its conventionality, language has to be learnt – we have to learn what members of a certain language community happen to call things, since there is no natural and universal way that words and sentences have to mean. Since language is productive, however, it cannot be the case that we learn English sentence by sentence. (Otherwise how could we understand new sentences as soon as we encounter them?) Instead, we must learn English recursively: We acquire a set of conventions that assign meanings to a finite stock of words and a set of rules for the combination of these words into an infinite number of sentences. In turn, this means that English is molecular – its sentences are built up from independently meaningful units – words or 'meaning atoms' – by rules that make the meaning of sentences depend on the meaning of their parts. And finally, since the meaning of a word is determined by convention and the meaning of a sentence is determined by the meanings of the words in it, literal meaning in our language is acontextual[116] – so the word 'horse' is always going to refer to the same kind of four-legged animal even if it acquires further connotations in specific linguistic contexts.

The next step is to consider whether film images possess these five interconnected, communicative features of a language. Since there is an unlimited number of things that can be conveyed by film images, advocates of film language are going to want to claim that film 'language' is productive. They also tend to emphasize its conventionality, though some more than others. Whereas Metz recognized that the depictive meaning of individual shots is natural and only insisted on denotative conventions for narrative meaning, another leading semiotician, Umberto Eco, insists that the conventions go all the way down, so to speak, determining the literal meaning of a single shot.[117] This is because even the most realistic and characteristic shot of an object does not reproduce the object exactly – three-dimensionality is lost, for example, on the screen. Therefore, for the viewer to recognize the object in the shot requires her to already know which features of an object are salient for its representation. And, according to Eco, we can only know this according to some kind of internalized convention. At this point, however, a problem arises. If we insist on the conventionality of film language along with its productivity, we are automatically committed to claiming that film language is recursive, molecular and acontextual. Unfortunately, this claim is false, which means that film images just don't work like a language.

There are no atoms of meaning for film images, since it is not the case that we understand a film image by understanding its parts and the rules according to which they are combined. A part of an image – say, a uniformly sandy part of an image of the Sahara in *Lawrence of Arabia* (1962) – just has meaning as a part and not independently of the whole. Although one could take parts of several images and combine them to make a new image, we surely do not want to say that every image is a collage or a composite in this way. Moreover, the parts of a composite image would still be parts of the original images from which they were extracted in the sense that they would not convey anything new in their new context – if we included the sandy image-part from *Lawrence of Arabia* in our composite image, that part of the new image would still just show sand. Thus image-parts are clearly not meaning atoms. But without meaning atoms, there is nothing to build up, according to rules, into a whole that is therefore meaningful both recursively and acontextually.

Insofar as we understand film images, it cannot be a result of our having acquired a lexicon of image-parts and having mastered rules for their grammatical combination. While we may not understand the dialogue in a Korean or a Turkish film without subtitles, we have no trouble making out the image track (assuming the images are in-focus and properly lit) even if what we make out includes unrecognizable objects and unfamiliar landscapes. What this suggests is that meaning in film, despite the standardization of film practice, is not conventional after all. For how could film language be productive, such that we recognize images we have never seen before, and still be conventional, given that we do not recognize new images as the result of their being built out of independently meaningful units according to rules? Currie argues that the productivity of film images has to be explained, not in terms of conventionality, but in terms of natural generativity. This notion is connected to Currie's argument for film realism that we discussed in Chapter 2. Just as with other kinds of picture, film images are understood insofar as we recognize what they depict in the same way as we would in real life. Thus we can understand new images insofar as we automatically and naturally recognize everything they show us.

Even if the meaning of film images is not determined conventionally, it can still be influenced by convention. After all, a filmed scene will look the way it does as a result of various conventions of dress, décor, and decorum. Objects within the filmed scene may have symbolic meaning – for instance, a crucifix, or a conventionally determined function – for instance, money. But none of these conventional influences mean that the image itself – like the word, 'horse,' is conventional. The problem, Currie suggests, with much of the semiotic theorizing about film, is that its conclusions about film language depend on glossing over this distinction and using the term 'convention' just as loosely and ambiguously as the term 'code'.

Given that film images lack important communicative features of language, Currie concludes that there is no language of film. This conclusion seems to foreclose the possibility of using linguistic analysis to solve the problem of film interpretation. However, it may be that this was never a real possibility in the first place. For, as Currie then goes on to suggest, even if there were a language of film, this would not wholly explain how we understand the story told by a film. Even though both words and images may have an acontextual, literal meaning, the former conventionally and the latter naturally, when either words or images are combined to make a narrative, context suddenly becomes highly important.

This is analogous to the importance of context in determining the meaning of utterances as opposed to the literal meaning of the words uttered. When you exclaim, 'I can't believe that this is happening to me!' or, 'My life sucks!', I have to know more than the literal meaning of the words you utter in order to know what you're talking about. I have to understand both the literal meaning of the words and the context in which you utter them – so, for example, I have to know what 'this' is that is happening to you or how your life can 'suck' but not in any literal way. Arguably, this is still a matter of literal meaning, but then we need a distinction between the literal meaning of the utterance, which depends on context, and the literal meaning of the string of words uttered, which does not. In literary works, context is even more important for understanding. For as well as understanding the context for particular utterances made by the characters or the narrator, we have to understand the narrative context of particular events so that we can figure out what is happening to the characters. Say we have a literary description of the heroine sipping some soup prepared by her jealous cousin immediately followed by a description of the heroine falling ill. We have to figure out whether the soup is the cause of her illness by making reference to what we already know about the story, especially the characters' motives.

The importance of context for narrative understanding is no less with film than with literature. If a shot of the heroine sipping her cousin's soup were immediately followed by a shot or sequence of the heroine falling ill, we would also have to figure out the relation between the depicted events by way of context. Recognizing what is depicted in the shots is only part of the process by which I come to understand the story. Thus a theory about how I come to recognize what is depicted in the shots will provide at best a partial explanation of narrative interpretation. In Chapter 6, we will examine more fully how film interpretation works. For now, it is enough to note that it is not just that there are problems with the analogy between film and language; there are also problems with the motivation for this analogy which is a solution to the problem of interpretation.

There may still be one final way to save the film-language analogy, however. What about the claim, not that film images themselves have a language-like structure, but that film images combine with one another in language-like ways? Is the meaning of certain standard shot combinations determined conventionally in just the same way as with sentential connectives? Take, as an example, the sentential connective, 'because'. When we join together two sentences, P and Q, with 'because,' there is a convention determining a literal meaning – that P is in some way a result of Q. But there is no analogous convention for determining that the event depicted in one shot is caused by the event depicted in the preceding shot. Rather, as with the example of the poisoned soup, we have to infer from the narrative context whether a particular pairing of shots indicates a causal relationship.

However, you might reply that even if there is no convention for signalling causation in a film, there are other conventions of editing that function like conventions determining the meaning of sentential connectives. Take, for example, shot/reverse-shot editing that combines a face-on shot of a character with a second shot from that character's point of view.[118] Given the frequent and standard use of this combination, is there a convention determining that any shot following a face-on shot of a character is from that character's point of view? No. In many instances, face-on character shots are not followed by point-of-view shots. But how, then, do we just seem to know when a shot following a face-on character shot is from that character's point of view?

It helps that shot/reverse-shot editing is used frequently in mainstream film. But, ultimately, we have to be paying attention to contextual cues. Perhaps, for example, the shot/reverse-shot combination is preceded by a medium-long shot of the character facing a certain scene, so that after the face-on shot, we know that the next shot showing the same scene from the character's perspective is a point-of-view shot. Or perhaps the shot/reverse-shot combination is part of a sequence that depicts two characters in conversation such that it is the dialogue that primarily cues the viewer to recognize a point of view. Whatever the particular contextual cues may be, the point is that we rely on such cues to understand the literal significance of an edited sequence in a way that we do not to understand the literal significance of sentential connectives.

Once again, therefore, film fails to exhibit a key feature of language – in this case, the acontextuality of the literal meaning of words. The example of shot/reverse-shot editing does not, however, suggest the complete absence of conventions governing the meaning of shot combinations in film. Metz's syntagmas and cases of film punctuation, like the fade in and out to indicate a significant passage of time, may still involve conventions. But even if there are a few conventions in film, they cannot function without individual shots already having a literal, natural meaning. Given the natural generativity of film images, we just don't need as many conventions to determine meaning in film except at the level of the ordering of images. At this level, conventions help constrain the interpretation of the film, which, Currie suggests, is the only way in which film conventions resemble language conventions.[119] But interpretation is a subject for another chapter.

CONCLUSIONS

In this chapter, we have examined the dangerous move from a metaphorical to a literal use of language terms in relation to film. Here is what we have covered:

1. Pudovkin's analogy between the shot and the word in terms of connotative meaning.
2. Eisenstein's analogy between a shot combination and an ideogram in terms of conceptual meaning.
3. Metz, Wollen and Eco's reduction of film analysis to a mysterious process of de-coding.
4. Currie's argument to show that film lacks the essential and interconnected communicative features of a natural language.
5. The further claim that, even if film were a language, this would not be enough to explain interpretation.

At this point, we might just content ourselves with saying that film is *like* a language in several ways – for example, in the way that some conventions play a role in constraining interpretation or in the way that film images are productive. But film is probably like a lot of other things in this same kind of loose and partial way. Ultimately, then, this kind of likeness is not enough to give us insight into the nature of film art.

CHAPTER 5

NARRATION IN THE FICTION FILM

As you may have noticed, the kind of film which has received the most attention from philosophers is narrative fiction film rather than, say, experimental non-narrative film or documentary. This is not surprising, perhaps, considering that most of the films most of us watch are narrative fiction films. In the simplest terms, a narrative film is a film that tells a story and a narrative *fiction* film is a film that tells a made-up story. This of course introduces the question of what counts as a made-up story and why, since not everything in a made-up story is made-up. But leaving this question aside, given that our interest is in a particular narrative art form, we need to think about what it really means to use moving images and sound to represent something that we then recognize as a story. The leading question for this chapter is, How does a film tell a story?

It is worth noting that in the history of film theory, this question has not been particularly central. The study of narrative is a well-established branch of literary theory, and as we shall see, some literary theorists extend their accounts of narrative to film. This indicates that the literary paradigm which influences discussions of film authorship and film language also influences discussions of film narration. In addition, some cognitive film theorists are interested in the psychological process of story comprehension. But the conceptual issues raised by the question of film narration have been of independent interest to philosophers. Thus the approach in this chapter is somewhat different than in previous chapters: We will not begin by trying to make sense of the film theory that deals with a particular philosophical issue but instead we will simply jump right to the current philosophical debate about particular aspects of narrative film.

There are many other kinds of narrative art besides film. There are novels, plays, epic poetry, ballet, opera, program music, comic strips and narrative painting and sculpture. Moreover, narrative is limited neither to art nor to fiction, since there are narratives of historical events and scientific discovery. On a minimal definition, a narrative is a chain of events, usually involving intentional action, which are ordered either temporally or causally. On a fuller definition, a narrative is also purpose-fully designed by someone to have a certain structure – a beginning, a middle, and an end – or a certain point – for example, entertainment.[120]

Note that the definition of narrative makes no reference either to medium or to content. As long as an artistic medium can represent a chain of events, it is a narrative medium. And regardless of what these events are, as long as they are ordered in a certain way, they are part of a narrative. This explains why the same story can be told in many forms – for example, the story of Dido and Aeneas told in an epic poem by Virgil, in a play by Christopher Marlowe and in an opera by Purcell; or the adaptation of Jane Austen's *Pride and Prejudice* for a television series and for the Bollywood film, *Bride and Prejudice* (2004).

Even though narrative is independent of particular artistic media, it seems likely that there are differences in narrative communication across media. In other words, the story of Dido and Aeneas is going to come over a little differently as an opera and as an epic poem. There is thus an interesting question about the distinctive features of narration in film, whether in the traditional medium of film or in video or digital media.

In order to come to an understanding of film narration, we will con-sider the following three questions:

1. Must narrative films always have narrators?
2. What is it for a film's narration to be unreliable?
3. How do films support narrative comprehension?

These are the main questions about film narration that concern phi-losophers and cognitive film theorists. The first two questions are often motivated by an interest in the possibility of structural similarities between narration in film and in literature. Thus the first question is often taken as shorthand for a more focused question: Given that literary fictions always or almost always have narrators, must fiction films, too, always have narrators? Similarly, the second question is often under-stood as a question about whether the same forms of narrative unreli-ability are found in film and in literature. Even when theorists approach the first two questions with reference to literature, however, they end up drawing attention to the remarkable variety of strategies available to a film-maker for keeping the audience interested in how the story goes. The third question then reminds us that whether a film's narrative strat-egy is effective greatly depends on the viewer.

To a large extent, we will consider the second and third questions in relation to the first. Our answer to the first question will be that narrative films may have but need not have narrators. Given this answer, and given that narrative unreliability is often accounted for in terms of the activity of a narrator, part of what will concern us in taking up the second question is whether there can be unreliable narration without a narrator. When it comes to the third question, we will focus on how we should divide up the work involved in following a story between the narrator, if there is one, and the viewer. A broader and more detailed analysis of the activity of narrative comprehension will be reserved for the next chapter, since narrative comprehension is one aspect of our cognitive-perceptual engagement with film. Overall, most of our attention in this chapter will be focused on the elusive figure of the cinematic narrator.

MUST NARRATIVE FILMS ALWAYS HAVE NARRATORS?

In general terms, a narrator is a fictional agent who tells a story, be it in a film, a novel, or a play. The narrator is part of the work of fiction, and most commonly, she reports or presents the story events that unfold in the work as though they actually happened. Sometimes, however, a narrator tells a fictional story, in which case, since the narrator is still part of the work, it is fictional that she is actually telling us a fiction. In either case, however, the task of the narrator, fictionally at least, is to report or present story events to the audience.

One motivation for arguing that films and other kinds of narrative artworks always have narrators is the observation that a story is always told in a certain way. This accounts for the tone of a work, or the set of attitudes manifest in the way that characters and events are described or depicted. The tone of a film is the result of a wide variety of stylistic choices concerning lighting, cinematography, *mise en scène*, and editing of both the image and sound tracks. When we pick up on the attitudes manifest in a film's style, we naturally want to assign these attitudes to someone. And if we want to assign them to someone inside the fiction, we assign them to a narrator.

There are in fact several kinds of narrator in film and when theorists argue about the necessity of a narrator, they are arguing about one particular kind. This kind of narrator is usually referred to as the 'cinematic narrator' and can be distinguished from character narrators and voice-over narrators. As an audio–visual medium, film is like theatre and unlike literature in being able both to tell and to show a story.[121] This means that in film there can be both verbal and visual narrators. A verbal narrator is most commonly a voice-over narrator who introduces and explains past events in the fictional world of the film as we are fictionally shown those events on screen. This kind of narrator can be one of the characters, as in *Fight Club* (1999) or *Sunset Boulevard* (1950), or an impersonal and omniscient figure as in *Magnolia* (1999) or *The Naked City* (1948).

In films that use voice-over narration, it is often the case that we are simultaneously shown what is described by the verbal narrator. But in a few more unusual cases, verbal narration and visual narration come apart. What the film shows us may contradict or complicate the story we are being told in voice-over. We are forced to decide which version of the story to trust – the one we are shown or the one we are told, thus indicating a form of narrative unreliability unique to two-track media like film media. We will examine this and other forms of narrative unreliability in detail further ahead. Before we do, however, it is important to note the way in which the coming-apart of visual and verbal narration might serve to reveal the cinematic narrator. When we are shown something other than what we are told by a film, it is as though someone else besides the voice-over narrator is in control of the image track. But who? Some theorists say it must be an implicit and exclusively visual narrator. In other words, someone whose presence is not explicitly signalled in the film but rather implied by the way that story events are shown.

This someone is the cinematic narrator, the fictional agent that certain theorists take to be part of the very structure and fabric of the narrative process. The most common conception of the cinematic narrator, and the conception that is assumed in most arguments against the cinematic narrator, is of the narrator as a guide to the events depicted on screen. Other more controversial conceptions include the narrator as witness[122] and the narrator as an 'image-maker'.[123] The difference between the conception of the narrator as a guide and the conception of the narrator as an image-maker is primarily a difference in what the narrator is taken to be presenting, whether the fictional events themselves or recorded images of those fictional events (instead of recorded images of the actual, staged events representing the fictional events).[124] The appeal of the conception of the narrator as guide is that it accommodates the way in which the frame of the shot seems to be used to point to the depicted events. However, some theorists question whether it is really a narrator, and not just an implied author, who is doing the pointing.

In Chapter 3, we learnt that an implied author is the person to whom we imaginatively attribute a work of art in order to make sense of that work in interpretation. A sufficiently unified film that was in fact made by a diverse group of artists and artisans could nevertheless be assigned a single, implied author in interpretation. It is important to distinguish between the implied author and the narrator since they stand in different relations to the story. The implied author is the agent to whom we attribute the whole work which happens to tell a fictional story. The narrator is part of this work and connected to the story in a particular way. The events of the story are always fictional for the implied author whereas they are usually real for the narrator.

If we are to conceive of the cinematic narrator as a guide, we need to ask whether his role can be distinguished from that of the implied author. The literary theorist Seymour Chatman is one of the leading defenders of the necessary role of a guiding narrator in narrative film.[125] He assumes that when we watch a film we imagine a narrator presenting the fictional events that are shown in the implied author's selected images. Further ahead, we shall see that other theorists question Chatman's assumption that selection and presentation are carried out by different agents. But first we need to consider Chatman's argument for the necessity of the cinematic narrator which has become standard in the literature. This argument has been called the a priori argument[126] because it is presented as simply elucidating how we use the concepts of narration and the narrator without relying on any empirical assumptions about the narrative arts. The basic idea is that there cannot be narration without a narrator because the one is conceptually dependent on the other. Here's one way the argument could go:

1. Narration is the activity of telling or showing a story.
2. Every activity has an agent.
3. The agent of the narration of a fictional story is the narrator.

So,

4. all narrative fictions, including all narrative fiction films, have narrators.

The most common objection to the a priori argument is that it doesn't prove what it aims to prove because the third premise involves an unwarranted assumption. It follows from the first and second premises of the argument that there must be a narrating agent. But this agent cannot be fictional, as the third premise claims, because the narration is a real thing:

A narrative film, for example, is an actual story-telling and -showing. The people responsible for making the film are the ones who are necessary for there to be an activity of narration, even if it is the narration of fictional events.

Another objection to the a priori argument concerns the assumption behind the second premise, that every activity has an agent by definition. Is this really true? Sometimes when we talk about an activity, we do not mean to imply the necessary presence of an agent – as when an astronomer remarks, 'there's a lot of activity in the sky tonight'. Why couldn't narration be this kind of agent-free activity? Clearly, the defender of the a priori argument has her work cut out for her.

The a priori argument is by no means the only argument for the necessity of the cinematic narrator. There is also an argument concerning how we come to know about the fictional world of a film, or more specifically, who is responsible for giving us a fictional view into this world.[127] This argument begins with the assumption that it is reasonable for the film viewer to ask about the means of perceptual access to a film's world. By way of an answer, the argument then claims that whoever gives us access to the fictional world of the film has to be part of that world. This is because only someone on the same ontological level as the characters and events of the story could present those characters and events as real.[128] Whereas the film-maker (or implied author) presents the story as a fiction, the narrator on the inside presents the events and characters of the story just as they are – in a novel this is achieved with the use of declarative sentences and in a film this is achieved just by showing the represented events and characters directly on screen. Thus in answer to the viewer's starting question about means of access, the argument purports to show that, since it cannot be the film-maker that provides access, it has to be the cinematic narrator.

In responding to this argument, we need to ask two questions: (1) Is it really *that* reasonable to expect an answer to the question of who is giving us a view into the fictional world of the film? And even if it is reasonable, (2) is it really the case that positing a narrator solves the problem of access? In answer to the first question, it might be unreasonable to ask about means of access because it is one of the conventions of fiction that we overlook inconsistent or paradoxical implications of the origins of the fictional narration. Take the example of the film, *American Beauty* (1999), which begins with voice-over narration by a dead character. If we felt compelled, in watching this film, to figure out how we are being told about the fictional events of the story, we would no doubt find ourselves confused or distracted. Similarly, if we stopped to figure out how we are being shown Charles Foster Kane alone on his deathbed in the dramatic opening scene of *Citizen Kane* (1941), we would also get nowhere. The point is that we don't have to start figuring this out and, in fact, many works of fiction require us not to in order to engage properly with the story. How we come to be told about or shown fictional events simply remains indeterminate in the fiction.

In answer to the second question about whether positing a narrator solves the problem of access, it is not clear how a fictional agent can present the fictional world of a film to a real audience. The argument suggests that the film-maker cannot give us access to the fictional world of the film because he is on a different ontological level from the film characters and events. But the narrator is on a different ontological level from us. So the same difficulty faces the narrator as the film-maker: How is the narrator supposed to bridge the ontological gap, assuming there is one, between the real world and the fictional world of the film in order to provide access?[129]

The question of the relation between the real and the fictional is also raised in an independent argument against the necessity of the cinematic narrator as guide. One way of construing this argument is as a challenge to a crucial assumption behind the a priori argument. Remember that the a priori argument claims that there must be an agent carrying out the activity of narration. The reason that this agent must be the narrator is because the events being narrated are fictional. Thus the assumption is that only a fictional agent can show us fictional events. The argument against fictional showing, as we shall call it, challenges this assumption: Just because you have the narration of fictional events doesn't mean that you have to have a fictional narration of those events by a fictional agent (the narrator).[130]

While it is true that only a fictional agent can show us the story events as actual, this does not rule out the possibility of the real author showing us the story events as fictional. What is more, the predominance of third-person, omniscient narrative style in various artistic media and genres might show how this possibility is realized. When someone tells a bedtime story to a child or repeats a ghost story round the campfire, he is the only one narrating – unless, of course, he is telling a story of the telling of story events. Similarly, when I decide to show you a fictional story in pictures, comic-strip style, unless I draw the pictures so as to represent, say, the eye-witness record of a fictional agent, I am the only one doing the showing. Nicholas Wolsterstorff makes the point in the following way.

> Presumably not all human narration consists of narrating what someone narrated. Why then must fictional narration have this structure? Why can't the novelist just straightforwardly tell us a tale of love and death, birth and war, jealousy and endeavour? Why must his tale always be the tale of a *narration* of love and death, birth and war, jealousy and endeavour?[131]

This may confuse the issue, however. Someone who believes that every work of narrative fiction is narrated need not hold that the narration forms a part of or the subject of the story being narrated. The narration is not normally about the narration. An additional worry is that the argument against fictional showing cannot account for the way in which a work of fiction almost always presents the fictional as actual. Whereas the author can present the fictional as fictional – as the argument suggests – only a fictional agent like the narrator can present the fictional as actual. This is an important point and much contested by philosophers who are interested in the nature of fiction.[132] The debate about the nature of fiction is complex and separate from our principal concerns in this chapter. But it is important to note that the point just raised could suggest a qualification to the scope of the argument against fictional showing.

At the end of the day, although there is disagreement about the *necessity* of the cinematic narrator, hardly anyone denies the *possibility* of the cinematic narrator. This is partly because some films give us a strong sense of being guided in our view of fictional events by an invisible and effaced agent. Sometimes a film may deliberately signal the presence of such an agent by breaking with certain narrative conventions. For example, there is a scene in *Last Year at Marienbad* (1961), where the voice-over narrator instructs someone to show us a different location for the event being related. Who could it be that the voice-over narrator instructs? If it must be someone inside the fiction who is charged with showing us what happens, this sounds a lot like the cinematic narrator. Examples like this show us that we need to think about when it is useful for our making sense of film narration to posit a cinematic narrator. This will depend on the particular narration and whether it is constructed so as to imply the mediation of an implicit visual guide.

WHAT IS IT FOR A FILM'S NARRATION
TO BE UNRELIABLE?

Another reason why it is important to decide whether films must always have narrators is so that we can understand narrative unreliability in film. If, when watching a film, we have the sense that we're not being told the whole or the true story of events, say by a character narrator, then we are most likely identifying narrative unreliability. The standard definition of narrative unreliability in literary theory invokes a narrator who intends to have us believe something other than what the (implied) author intends to be true in the fiction. Given the discussion we have just had about whether every film has a narrator, the interesting question is whether you can have narrative unreliability without a narrator. If you can, then the possibility of narrative unreliability cannot be assumed to support any necessary claims about the narrator.

Even if it is true that in literature unreliable narration is always the work of an unreliable narrator, this does not automatically account for the case of film. This is because film, in its capacity both to tell and to show a story, can be unreliable in unique and distinctive ways. Two-track unreliability can take different forms, depending on how a particular film sets up a tension between verbal and visual narration. In more unusual cases, even though verbal narration and visual narration are uniformly consistent, a film may exhibit a subtle form of global unreliability. This kind of unreliability is revealed by ambiguity in the interpretation of a film and can be described without reference to a narrator.

Two-track Unreliability

Two-track unreliability usually involves a voice-over narrator telling us a different story from the one being shown. It depends on the film as to whether it is the verbal or visual version of the story that is the true (or 'truer') version. But it is most common for the visual version to be true, most likely because we have a tendency to trust what we see over what we are told. Films narrated in voice-over by a child or a slow-witted adult like Forrest Gump will often show more than the verbal narrator understands to tell. More unusual cases where we are supposed to trust what we are told over what we are shown include films which blur or obscure our fictional view of events for particular emotional effect and then help us follow those events with voice-over explanation.

Sometimes verbal and visual narration only come apart at certain points in a film or part-way through a film. This shift serves to draw attention to the possibility of unreliable narration and to prompt the viewer to pay careful attention to how the story unfolds. Although most commonly the point at which visual and verbal narration come apart is the point at which unreliability begins, more unusually, it can also be the point at which prior unreliability is revealed and comes to an end. This involves the visual narration, up to a certain point in the film, having corroborated an unreliable verbal narration, or vice-versa. Recent films that employ this strategy include *A Beautiful Mind* (2001) and *Sixth Sense* (1999). But the most famous example is *Stage Fright* (1950).

In this film, Johnny is suspected by the police of killing his lover's husband. His friend Eve offers to hide him and Johnny explains to her that his lover is the real murderer. Eve decides to investigate for herself, however, and soon learns that Johnny has been lying to her. But when Johnny is telling Eve his version of the murder, the image-track corroborates by showing his lover committing the murder. This makes it a surprise to learn along with Eve that Johnny was lying. It is only when Eve starts investigating for herself that we learn that the narration of the murder flashback was unreliable. Interestingly, the film received a great deal of criticism for its use of unreliable narration. This was because the film brings the audience to trust Johnny's version of events by providing a visual exposition of his verbal narration. There is something particularly unsettling about discovering that one has been deceived by what one sees as well as by what one is told.

Global Unreliability

Global unreliability is found only in films with a particular kind of complex narrative structure. It is not based on a tension between showing and telling, or on a marked shift away from a faithful showing of a character's voice-over narration. Instead, this kind of unreliability characterizes the entire narrative process of a film and only becomes evident through questions of story interpretation. George Wilson claims that *You Only Live Once* (1937) exhibits global unreliability. In the film, Eddie, a former criminal, is accused of carrying out a fatal robbery and sentenced to death on circumstantial evidence. At the last minute, however, following the apprehension of a new suspect, he is granted a pardon. Unfortunately, Eddie is already involved in a prison break, and interpreting his pardon as a trick, kills the prison chaplain. The delivery of Eddie's pardon, combined with the sympathetic treatment of his character, make it clear to most viewers that Eddie is innocent of the fatal robbery. However, Wilson suggests that on closer inspection the film makes Eddie's innocence an open question for the viewer that ultimately cannot be answered. This is because the robbery is shown in a highly ambiguous way so that we cannot say for sure who is involved. The film's narration is unreliable because it initially encourages us to accept Eddie's innocence but not without introducing various incongruities that undermine any final judgment. In other words, the narration itself suggests an initial interpretation of the story which obscures the correct interpretation.

Unlike the first kind of narrative unreliability, global unreliability need not involve an explicit, verbal narrator. Of course it could be claimed that this kind of unreliability still depends on the work of a narrator; just an implicit one. It is not easy to support this claim, however, because of the fact that to judge an agent to be unreliable requires knowing something about her personality and we don't know anything of the personality of an implicit narrator just because he is implicit. Perhaps, then, it would be easier to try to account for this kind of unreliability without reference to a narrator. Gregory Currie does just this when he gives an account of complex narrative unreliability exclusively in terms of the intentions of the implied author.[133] According to Currie, the implied author can intend for the images and sounds of the film to be taken one way on a superficial interpretation and another way on a deeper, more reflective interpretation. In the case of *You Only Live Once*, since it is the film as a whole that supports a second, conflicting interpretation of the events portrayed, and the film is seen as the work of the implied author, only the implied author – and not someone inside the fiction – can be responsible for its unreliability .

Where narrative unreliability is the result of tension between a character's telling and the showing of story events, we should not assume that this amounts to a conflict between two narrators, one explicit and verbal, the other implicit and visual. As we have seen, some theorists think that visual narration, even when it is a narration of fictional events, can be directly attributed to the implied author. Where narrative unreliability does not involve the activity of an explicit, verbal narrator, we also cannot assume that some other kind of narrator must be involved, specifically, an implicit, visual narrator. As Currie's account suggests, such cases may be best accounted for in terms of the complex intentions of the implied author. Thus if, as suggested earlier, we should be interested primarily in the interpretive function of positing the cinematic narrator, when we are trying to understand the subtle forms of narrative unreliability that are distinct to film, we may not wish to mention the cinematic narrator at all.

Cases like *You Only Live Once* draw our attention to the fact that narrative unreliability takes more or less complex forms. Moreover, it may be that only complex forms of narrative unreliability are of real theoretical interest. This is Currie's suspicion based on the fact that we don't assume that narrators are always reliable in the first place. It is thus particularly when we are led to trust in the reliability of a film's narration – whether or not it involves a narrator – only then to discover that the narration is unreliable in some way, that we become aware of new possibilities for narration in film.

HOW DO FILMS SUPPORT
NARRATIVE COMPREHENSION?

The case of unreliable narration draws our attention to the work of the viewer in making sense of the story because the function of unreliability very much depends on how and when the viewer is supposed to pick up on it. This brings us to our last question about narrative comprehension. The way in which this question has been framed in the literature is in terms of how much work the narration leaves up to the viewer. In particular, theorists are interested in whether a film's narration directs the viewer to construct the full story herself rather than having it provided entirely by the sounds and images on screen.

There are important links between narration, the narrator, and narrative comprehension. Depending on how one conceives of narration, or the narrative process as a whole, one will be more or less inclined to insist on the necessity of the narrator. And depending on whether one insists on the necessity of the narrator, one will be more or less comfortable with assigning a role for the viewer in narrative construction. Remember that Chatman comes to the conclusion that every work of narrative fiction, including every narrative fiction film, has a narrator because narration is an activity carried out by an agent. More specifically, Chatman conceives of narration as a complex communicative activity whereby the narrator as communicator conveys a story to his audience. This is not the only way of conceiving of narration, however. The leading cognitive film theorist, David Bordwell, rejects Chatman's conclusions about the role of the narrator in part because he rejects Chatman's conception of narration as communication.[134] Moreover, Bordwell conceives of narration in a way that implies an active role for the viewer in shaping the narrative.

In order for the narrator to play the role that some theorists assign to him, the whole story has to be present in the film – only then can the narrator serve to tell or show the story from the inside. Bordwell doesn't think that the whole story is in the film. In fact, he doesn't think that any of the story is in the film because he thinks that the viewer constructs the story herself. First, Bordwell marks a distinction between plot and story, for which he borrows the terms *syuzhet* and *fabula* from the Russian formalists, a group of literary theorists active between 1914 and 1930 who Bordwell claims were the first to fully theorize the distinction between the narrative and narration.[135] The *syuzhet*, or plot, as the actual presentation and arrangement of story events in the film cues the viewer to construct the *fabula*, or story.[136] In other words, the viewer makes inferences from what she is shown on screen, together with her background knowledge of the world and film culture, in order to arrive at a coherent picture of 'what really happened' in the film – a chronological, causal chain of events.[137]

This may sound more mysterious a process than it really is. With his extensive knowledge of the psychology of film-viewing and film form, Bordwell is just building on the observation that no film gives us everything in terms of a story. We have to assume that characters don't cease to exist in the fictional world of the film when the actors walk off screen. We have to assume that a whole night has passed when we are shown two consecutive shots of a character lying down to sleep in darkness and awakening in daylight. And we have to assume the correct order of events in a character's life even when we are shown his childhood in flashback from his deathbed. These are just three examples of the multitude of assumptions about story events that we make in watching a film. Such examples suggest that it is false to think of the film viewer as a passive recipient of a fully worked-out and comprehensible story from an active and controlling narrator. If story comprehension is constructive as Bordwell claims, then an advocate of the cinematic narrator would have to rethink the narrator's role. Perhaps the narrator gives us the narrative information out of which to construct a story; perhaps the narrator and the viewer enter into a collaboration for determining the whole story; or perhaps the viewer takes over the role of the narrator in this process.

The question of whether the viewer constructs the story is a much more complicated one than we have made it sound here. This is partly because, for Bordwell at least, the question is attached to a much broader constructivist theory which applies to every level of engagement with film – from the most basic level of image recognition to the highest levels of interpretation and criticism. We will return to consider Bordwell's constructivist theory more closely in the next chapter. For now, let us keep in mind that we need to consider the activity of the viewer in following a film's story in order to understand more fully the nature of film narration.

CONCLUSIONS

As a final reminder, here are the main points we have covered in this chapter:

1. The status of the cinematic narrator; her relation to the story, to the implied author, and to the viewer.
2. Two standard arguments for the necessity of the cinematic narrator – that narration just is the activity of a narrator, and that only a narrator can give us access to fictional events.
3. Some compelling objections to these arguments concerning the status of the agent responsible for narration, and the indeterminacy of means of access to the fiction.
4. A further argument against the necessity of the cinematic narrator that challenges the assumption that fictional events can only be shown by a fictional agent.
5. Complex forms of two-track narrative unreliability only possible in film and not in literature.
6. The possibility of global narrative unreliability without a narrator.
7. The implications of positing a narrator for our understanding of the process of narrative comprehension – in particular, whether the viewer passively receives the story from a narrator or actively constructs the story.

In this chapter we have raised doubts about the necessity of the cinematic narrator. As we discovered, this has considerable implications for our understanding of narrative unreliability and narrative comprehension. We learnt that whereas unreliability in verbal narration may best be explained in terms of the intentions of a narrator, unreliability in visual narration may not be. This highlights the fact that, with both an image track and a sound track to manipulate through editing, filmmakers have a great deal of freedom in how they tell a story, perhaps more than in any other art form.

Given this freedom, we might expect that film narratives would be particularly hard to follow or engage with. This does not seem to be the case, however. If anything, film narratives are the most absorbing and accessible kind. The further question is what exactly is going on when we engage with a narrative film. Our work in this chapter suggests that it need not be due to the work of a narrator in supplying a pre-digested story that we are able to follow a film narrative. In the next chapter, we will see the extent to which it is up to us to bring the story together, and how much of the work assigned to a narrator in guiding us through fictional events could actually be assigned to the viewer.

CHAPTER 6

THE THINKING VIEWER

The experience of watching a film, especially a popular, mainstream film, can feel effortless and absorbing. However, in some ways, this is deceptive, since the ease of the experience is facilitated by our performing a large number of complex cognitive activities. If we are watching a narrative fiction film, for example, we have to figure out what's going on in the story. This sounds simple enough and yet requires us to perceive movement, recognize what is being depicted on screen, interpret characters' behaviour, make causal connections and more generally fill gaps in the narrative, form expectations about what will happen next, and keep track of spatial and temporal configurations within the film's fictional world. Moreover, the viewer's cognitive activity does not end when the film ends.

After we have left the cinema or turned off the television, we may start wondering about the film's deeper meaning, its themes, moral, or message – for example, what the film tells us about life and death, love, power, sexuality or even the nature of film itself. And even if we don't look for deeper meaning, we almost certainly form judgments about whether the film was any good, judgments that go beyond mere preference and aspire to objectivity. This suggests that there are three principal activities performed by the thinking film viewer: comprehension, interpretation, and evaluation. In this chapter, we will analyse each of these activities and thereby come to see that, although our cognitive engagement with film is rarely self-conscious, it is complex and varied. In other words, contrary to the familiar disparagement, there is nothing 'mindless' about the entertainment films provide.

NARRATIVE COMPREHENSION

Comprehension involves our figuring out what is going on in a film as we watch it. The most fully developed account of comprehension in relation to narrative film is the constructivist account given by the leading cognitive film theorist, David Bordwell.[138] On his account, comprehension is the activity of coming to grasp the literal meaning of a film. There are two kinds of literal meaning: referential meaning consists in the content of the fictional world – everything depicted, including temporal, spatial and causal relations that structure the narrative, and explicit meaning consists in a moral, message or theme explicitly signalled by the film.[139] The reason Bordwell labels his account 'constructivist' is that he takes the literal meaning of a film to be constructed by or projected onto the film by the viewer in response to the film's structural 'cues'.

Bordwell's constructivism is opposed to the traditional view that the viewer simply finds the meaning that is already there in a film. As we shall see, it is not just literal meaning that Bordwell takes to be constructed, but also the less obvious meanings that we grasp through interpretation. At the level of interpretation, there are, again, two kinds of meaning: Both implicit and symptomatic meaning are like explicit meaning in being general and abstract – indeed, the same moral, message, or theme could be any of the three kinds of meaning. The difference is in the relationship between the moral, message, or theme and the 'text' – whether the meaning is signalled explicitly or implicitly, or not intentionally signalled at all but rather symptomatic of, say, the dominant ideology or the film-maker's hang-ups.[140] Further ahead, we will examine Bordwell's account of interpretation as well as George Wilson's critique of Bordwell's distinction between comprehension and interpretation.[141] But first, we will see how Bordwell maps out a hierarchy of cognitive activities involved in comprehension, activities which are no less constructive for being primarily automatic, instantaneous, and unconscious.

At the most basic level, the very act of perceiving a film is constructive. Bordwell embraces the dominant view in cognitive psychology that perceiving an object does not just require passively receiving visual, aural or tactile data but also making an inference from the data in order to reach a perceptual judgment. Bordwell refers to such judgments as 'hypotheses' to suggest that perception is always open to revision in the face of new data or a new application of relevant background knowledge. Perceptual inferences can be made in two directions, either from the 'bottom up,' as in colour recognition where we draw a conclusion from the perceptual input, or from the 'top–down,' as in facial recognition where the perceptual data is largely organized by our expectations, background knowledge, and other cognitive activities.[142] In either case, however, whether the 'premises' of the inference derive from the perceptual input or from prior knowledge, it is up to the perceiver to reach a conclusion. In this sense, then, the perceiver makes what she perceives. Interestingly, film depends on our making the wrong inferences as a result of two physiological deficiencies in our visual systems.[143] In order to see a film as a sequence of continuously lit, moving images, we must make the wrong inferences from the data which consists in rapidly flashing light and a rapid display of static images. It is only because our eyes cannot keep up with the rapidity of changes, both in light intensity and in the image display, that a film is what it is experienced as; namely, a motion picture.

For most viewers familiar with the relevant representational, narrative, and cinematic conventions, once they have constructively perceived the two-dimensional image sequences projected on screen, it is just as automatic for them to construct a three-dimensional, fictional world from these images. This is not to say, however, that the second level of construction is straightforward. The viewer must draw on considerable background knowledge to determine the right configuration of three-dimensional objects shown in an inherently ambiguous two-dimensional image. This ambiguity derives from the fact that the same two-dimensional image could be an image of many arrangements of objects. For example, when we recognize an image of a 'costumed man' we have already disambiguated the image by imagining its object as a particular three-dimensional configuration – that of a costumed man. But instead of a costumed man, we could imagine 'a scatter of garments flung up and frozen, with a huge head miles off that happens to coincide, on our view, with the top edge of the collar'.[144] Indeed, if the image is a photograph, it could have been caused by either three-dimensional configuration.

Thus the process of disambiguating the image, while instantaneous and automatic, is still highly informed. But this is not the only process involved in constructing the three-dimensional world of the film. In addition, the viewer must draw on considerable background knowledge to determine the fictional state of affairs represented by the image. Part of constructing the fictional state of affairs is constructing its spatial and temporal parameters which extend beyond the image. When an actor walks out of the frame of the shot, for example, we do not think, without special reason, that her character has ceased to exist; rather we think that the character has moved into part of the fictional world that is not presently shown to us.

Insofar as the viewer is constructing fictional events and characters according to the order of images, she is constructing what Bordwell, following the Russian Formalists, calls the '*syuzhet*,' or 'plot'. As we learnt in the previous chapter, the *syuzhet* is the narrative just as it is shown on screen – as an incomplete and often out-of-order sequence of events. By filling in missing narrative information and re-ordering the depicted events into a causal sequence, the viewer then constructs the '*fabula*,' or 'story,' from the *syuzhet*. The difference between *fabula* and *syuzhet* can be seen when someone asks you to tell them what happens in a film.

In answering this question, you would not just describe what was depicted on screen in the order it was depicted, since the listener would quickly become lost. If, for example, your description began, 'All of Ralphie's family and friends are gathered by his graveside, then Ralphie steps on to a tram, then he orders lunch . . .', the listener would likely interrupt with a string of questions: 'How could Ralphie be dead one minute and then boarding a tram the next, and how could he be on the tram and then instantaneously at lunch? Surely you're not saying his ghost ordered lunch on the tram?' The listener is expecting you to have already done the work of re-ordering and filling in the story so that you can tell him that Ralphie rode a tram to his lunch destination, which led to some other event, which led to still others, which finally lead to Ralphie's death, indicated right at the beginning of the film but left unexplained until the very end. Thus what happens in a film is not just what happens on screen (and on the soundtrack). Rather, what happens in the film is an imaginatively filled in, re-ordered, and expanded version of what happens on screen.

The role of imagination is crucial in the film viewer's construction of the fictional world of the narrative and the narrative itself. We imagine that when we are looking at flat images on screen, we are watching fictional events occur in a three-dimensional world. We also imagine, but without imagining seeing, the off-screen space into which a character steps when the actor moves beyond the camera's view. And we imagine what happens between the shot of Ralphie stepping onto the tram and the shot of his ordering lunch; namely, that he takes the tram to his lunch destination. All of this suggests that although Bordwell takes himself to be giving a unified constructivist account of film-viewing, construction at the level of perception may be a different thing than construction at the level of *fabula* apprehension.[145] Perception is constructive because it involves the application of concepts to perceptual data in the making of inferences, not because we imagine what we perceive. It is important to keep in mind this distinction between construction as an inferential activity and construction as an imaginative activity because, when Bordwell proceeds to claim that interpretation, and not just comprehension, is constructive, he reverts to the perceptual model.

INTERPRETATION

Once the viewer has figured out what is going on in a film by constructing the *fabula*, she may wish to continue generating more abstract thematic and symptomatic meanings for the film. However, this is often an activity that only film scholars pursue. Indeed, this is often the only activity that film scholars pursue. As Bordwell and others point out, ever since its entrance into the academy, film studies has been heavily dominated by interpretation at the expense of analysis and evaluation. Moreover, the process by which academic critics interpret films has become highly regulated such that it is governed by institutional norms. But the interpretive process is still constructive just by being actively inferential.

On Bordwell's analysis, the critic maps concepts, which are structured as 'semantic fields,' onto those cues in a film that the critical tradition considers effective in viewers' comprehension and capable of bearing meaning. For example, critics inspired by psychoanalysis might set out to interpret a film in terms of the dual theme of voyeurism and fetishism, a theme that is recognized as significant within the community of critics. Such an interpretation would involve a highly selective treatment of the film in terms of particular suggestive features – say, camerawork that can be described as voyeuristic, or a contrast in characters' behaviour that can be described as symbolizing the voyeurism/fetishism duality. A certain theme becomes institutionally entrenched when it is flexible enough to be used in many contexts. For example, the auteurists favoured the theme of confession since it allows the critic to tie together disparate scenes across a director's body of work involving confession of any kind – legal, religious, or personal, and then, perhaps, to tie these scenes of confession to the 'confessional' style of the director. The process of mapping semantic fields onto cues is aided by 'socially implanted hypotheses about how texts mean,' in particular the hypotheses that the text is unified and that it is related to an external world.[146] In other words, the critic assumes that he can draw on background knowledge about the world around him to make sense of the film as something with a single, overall meaning.

The mapping process is achieved by the employment of heuristics, standard rules of thumb which have proved useful in generating novel and plausible interpretations. One popular heuristic is the punning heuristic, which involves, for example, taking the depiction of passageways in a film to suggest that the film is about the 'passage' of life, or taking the framing of certain shots to indicate that the film is about the 'framing' of innocents. Once the critic has settled on and refined her semantic fields, and organized their application to suggest an overall meaning for the film, she must write up her interpretation in a way that is recognized as suitably persuasive by the interpretive institution. Not surprisingly, perhaps, Bordwell's analysis of interpretation as highly standardized has been very unpopular among academic critics who do not like to think of themselves as assembly-line workers in 'Interpretation, Inc'. However, a deeper criticism of Bordwell's analysis can be found by examining his prior commitment to constructivism.

Although, as we have seen, there may be more than one version of constructivism at work in Bordwell's account, one basic idea is that the film viewer's activities are constructive insofar as they are inferential and involve the application of concepts. Since perception, narrative comprehension, and interpretation are all constructive processes, Bordwell assumes that their objects are constructs. Hence his famous statement, 'Meanings are not found but made'.[147] Unfortunately, however, as Berys Gaut points out, Bordwell is making a false assumption. The fact that perception is an active, inferential process does not mean that the objects of perception – namely the things we perceive around us – are constructed. After all, one can think that the external world we perceive is really there and yet still think that the mind's activities are constructive. Furthermore, a critic who thinks, contra Bordwell, that meanings are not made but found in the film can still allow that the process of finding them is active and inferential.

This same critic can also allow that interpretation is governed by institutional norms, since many forms of detection, including criminal and scientific investigation, occur within institutions and yet retain independent objects of inquiry. Further evidence against interpretive constructivism is suggested by the fact that interpretation is constrained, not by the norms of the interpretive institution as Bordwell suggests, but by the norms of the film and its generative context. A critic who fails to understand how certain techniques were standardly used in a particular filmmaking tradition is likely to misinterpret their significance in a film which is part of that tradition. Whereas, for example, a critic would be right to interpret low-angle shots in *Citizen Kane* as connoting the power or threat of a dominant character (or, in certain scenes, as connoting lost power and pathetic isolation[148]), he would be wrong to interpret low-angle shots in *Rashomon* (1950) in the same way. This is because, in classical Japanese filmmaking, the low-angle shot simply captures the perspective of someone seated on a *tatami* mat and has no special expressive force.[149] If the critic were the one constructing significance, there would be no possibility of her being wrong about the meaning of low-angle shots in *Rashomon*. The fact that she can be wrong indicates that the norms governing interpretation are not the norms internal to critical practice but the external norms of artistic and filmmaking traditions, and social practices.

Thus it seems that interpretation is not constructive in the way that Bordwell suggests. Interestingly, however, this criticism may not stick, since it is unclear whether Bordwell actually endorses the kind of interpretation he analyses. He may simply be describing the way things are done in film studies while recognizing that constructive interpretation is incoherent – a critic may in fact proceed as if it is entirely up to him what a film means when in fact this is not the case. Bordwell may wish to reveal what is really going on in academic criticism in the hope of undermining current practice. This reading of Bordwell's aims is supported by the fact that he also calls for a redress of the imbalance in favour of interpretation that has characterized contemporary film studies.

As an alternative to narrowly interpretive film analysis, Bordwell recommends a 'historical poetics' of film which is in fact sensitive to the kind of historical and social norms that properly constrain interpretation. This approach involves analysing how films work – how they are put together technically and formally to achieve certain ends (say, to tell a story or embody certain meanings) and to prompt a certain kind of active engagement on the part of the viewer. The reason that Bordwell considers his poetics to be 'historical' is because it involves recognition of the fact that films work differently in different contexts – as part of different filmmaking and broader artistic traditions, or when viewed by different kinds of audience at different times.[150]

The ambiguity of Bordwell's aims in giving an account of film interpretation affects the force of another line of criticism. George Wilson argues that interpretation is more than Bordwell claims, since there is a kind of interpretation that is continuous with comprehension. But if Bordwell's account of interpretation is merely descriptive rather than prescriptive, Bordwell can respond simply by arguing that this other kind of interpretation which Wilson identifies happens not to have been part of the academic tradition to which Bordwell's stipulative distinction between comprehension and interpretation applies. Wilson in fact acknowledges that Bordwell may be happy to prescribe this other, neglected kind of interpretation as part of a poetics of film. But even if Wilson does not undermine Bordwell's account of the current state of interpretation, he draws our attention to the fact that taking interpretation to be concerned with messages and themes may involve a problematic linguistic conception of narrative meaning to which there is an alternative; namely, narrative meaning as the causal significance of events.

According to Wilson, there is a kind of interpretation concerned, not with abstract themes and messages, but with a more nuanced grasp of the referential meaning of a film. This kind of interpretation does not rely on any specialized theoretical skills and remains open to rational criticism by those outside particular critical schools. This is because it draws on the ordinary cognitive skills, and the norms governing their application, that we employ when trying to make sense of puzzling events in our lives. We find meaning in, or give meaning to, such events by connecting them to other events so that they have a significant place in a narrative framework or causal pattern. Similarly, when we are watching narrative fiction films, we are often left with questions as to why the story took the turn it did at a particular point, or why a character behaved a certain way in a certain scene. In order to answer these questions, we may have to look more closely at the details of the narrative, and in so doing, we may make different connections between events, or weigh events differently.[151] As a result, we may find that the events of the film tell a slightly different, and perhaps better, story than the one that we understood on first viewing. Alternatively, we might find that the film does not tell a consistent story at all and thus exhibits one of the forms of narrative unreliability discussed in the previous chapter. This kind of interpretation is essentially reflective comprehension that draws on more complex evidence and pays more attention to the broader narrative context than ordinary comprehension, but nevertheless relies on the same skills in making causal judgments.

The norms that determine the reasonableness of our judgments about real-life causes and effects carry over to our judgments about causes and effects in a film's fictional world – that is, unless it is clear that causality works differently in a particularly strange fictional world. Given the universality of these norms, interpretations involving causal explanation need not be relativized to a particular academic practice involving the use of characteristic semantic fields and heuristics. We do not need to be part of such a practice, familiar with all its acceptable moves and theoretical assumptions, to give this kind of interpretation. We do, however, need to be skilled at noticing anomalous narrative elements and scrutinizing the film in order to integrate these elements into a significant causal pattern. This takes practice, but not at the tricks of the academic interpretative trade. Rather, it takes practice simply at watching films well.

In closing our discussion of interpretation, it is worth noting that while film scholars may be centrally, or even exclusively, concerned with the deeper meaning of films, ordinary viewers tend to skip from ordinary comprehension to evaluation. As long as we are able to follow a film, or sometimes even precisely because we are unable to follow it, we usually emerge from the cinema eager to share our opinions about whether the film in question was any good.

EVALUATION

Have you noticed how much we talk about the films we see and how much of our talk involves evaluating these films? If you tell a friend that you have just seen a new film, there is a good chance that her first question will be, 'Was it any good?' Even if your friend does not know what the film is about, she may still ask for your evaluation before or without asking for a plot or thematic synopsis. It is, moreover, revealing to think about ways in which you might answer your friend's question. You could say, 'Well, no, the film wasn't that good, but I still liked it'. This implies that film evaluation is not just the registering of preferences, likes and dislikes. Similarly, if you had answered just by saying, 'Well, I liked it,' the fact that your friend could then repeat her question – 'OK, but was it any good?' – indicates that film evaluation, like art evaluation in general, aims at objectivity. This is also supported by the way you could follow up your initial answer by giving reasons for your evaluation, reasons which are grounded in intersubjectively verifiable facts. If you had answered your friend by saying, 'Yes, the film was brilliant,' or 'No, the film was bad,' it is also likely that she would not be satisfied until you gave reasons for such an evaluation.

But suppose you went to see the film with your cousin, and when your friend asks whether the film was any good, you and your cousin give opposite answers. While you say the film was good, your cousin says it was terrible, and neither of you take yourself merely to be stating a preference. Upon discovering that you and your cousin have reached different conclusions about the film, you need not simply shrug and say, 'oh well, he and I often like different things'. Instead, you could proceed to argue with your cousin in the hope of convincing him, through the presentation of reasons, to change his mind. But is this a false hope? Can we really expect to resolve disagreements about whether a film is good or bad? According to Noël Carroll, a theory of film evaluation addresses just these questions, thereby aiming to account for the possibility of the rational resolution of disagreement.[152]

Before we examine the details of Carroll's own theory of evaluation, we should note that even though all of us like to evaluate the films we see, professional critics still serve a number of useful functions. They can help us select which films to watch, either by identifying films which match our current tastes or by making a case for the merits of a film that we would otherwise have skipped. In addition, critics can prepare us to defend our evaluations more effectively, including when we defend our evaluations against the critics themselves in imaginary conversations sparked by reading film reviews.[153] Finally, Carroll suggests a way in which critics can help us resolve a certain kind of evaluative disagreement; the kind involving a category error. Critics can introduce us to new kinds of films, thereby enabling us to place a film in the correct category and evaluate it according to the standards of that category. This raises questions about what it means to categorize a film, how we know we have categorized a film correctly, and why a correct categorization might support an evaluation that we can agree on. To answer these questions, we need to examine Carroll's 'Pluralistic Category Approach' to film evaluation.

Although there are various kinds of evaluative disagreement, Carroll suspects many disagreements could be resolved if the film in question were placed in the right category or categories. A category can be a genre, a movement, a school, or a style, which is not necessarily specific to film. To take a simple example, suppose that your cousin complains about the lack of explosions in *Four Weddings and a Funeral* (1994). By pointing out that the film is a romantic comedy, you undermine the criticism and open the way for a discussion of the merits of the film relative to, say, *The Wedding Crashers* (2005) or *Annie Hall* (1977). Precisely because these other films are of the same kind as *Four Weddings and a Funeral*, they share some of the same general aims – for example, the aims of being funny and making us root for the principal romantic couple. It is simply unfair to condemn *Four Weddings and a Funeral* for a lack of explosions, since having explosions is not essential to meeting the aims of this particular subgenre. Of course, a romantic comedy could have an explosion, which could either serve a comedic or romantic purpose, or serve some other purpose not specific to the genre. This indicates that we are not limited to evaluating films by category, and even when we do evaluate films in this way, we are not thereby ignoring the unique ways in which particular films fulfil the purposes of their categories.

It is not just a matter of personal opinion as to how a film is to be categorized. Carroll names three kinds of objective reason for placing a film in a certain category: (1) structural reasons, (2) intentional reasons and (3) contextual reasons.[154] There are structural reasons for categorizing *Four Weddings and a Funeral* as a romantic comedy insofar as the film has many characteristic features of the subgenre, including witty dialogue, a sympathetic yet amusingly incompetent romantic hero, and a happy ending involving romantic reconciliation. In addition, there is good evidence, both manifest in the work – say, in the dialogue and choice of actors – and outside the work – say, in interviews, that the makers of *Four Weddings and a Funeral* intended the film to be a romantic comedy. And finally, there is some contextual evidence for the categorization, since romantic comedy is the favoured subgenre of Richard Curtis, the writer of *Four Weddings and a Funeral*, as well as a staple of mainstream, narrative film.

As our example suggests, structural, intentional, and contextual reasons often converge in supporting a particular categorization. The fact that Richard Curtis is the writer of *Four Weddings and a Funeral* suggests an intentional reason for the categorization, and in general, context can be a clue to intentions, since filmmakers tend to want to make films in categories that are familiar to the audience. Similarly, structural considerations can be a clue to intentions – as above, where the dialogue seems deliberately crafted for romance and comedy. Despite this convergence, however, one kind of reason alone may be sufficient to justify a particular categorization, particularly when there are no good reasons for an alternate categorization.[155]

In sum, Carroll aims to show that the rational resolution of evaluative disagreements about films is possible, at least when the disagreements in question are the result of a category error which we can work to correct by the citing of structural, intentional, and contextual evidence. In recommending categorical evaluation as a primary form of film criticism, Carroll also anticipates and responds to a number of potential objections.[156]

Categorical evaluation, Carroll insists, is neither narrowly aesthetic nor inherently conservative. It is not narrowly aesthetic because some categories have cognitive, political, or ethical aims, or aims that depend on cognitive, political, or ethical criteria. And it is not inherently conservative, or insensitive to the historical progression of filmmaking, because there are various ways in which we can understand new categories almost as soon as they emerge. Carroll also maintains that a film that cannot be categorized is highly unlikely, and indeed, such a film would be unintelligible. This is not to say, however, that every film can be easily categorized and indeed, as noted above, one task for the professional critic is to introduce us to the more obscure and unfamiliar categories into which unusual films fit. Finally, Carroll recognizes that categorical evaluation will be complicated, since many films belong to multiple categories and meet the aims of each category with varying success.

It is important to note that Carroll is not claiming that correct categorization will end all disagreement about the value of a film. We may be able to agree on which categories a film belongs to and yet be unable to agree on the standards, and weighting of those standards, for the categories in question.[157] Furthermore, even if we successfully make the move from correct categorization to shared evaluation, still other kinds of evaluative disagreement may persist. For example, we might disagree about whether a film's twisted plot structure is effective or simply confusedly contrived, whether a certain actor was the right choice for the protagonist, whether the film's special effects are convincing, whether a film's style of camerawork or lighting, or its colour palette, are arresting or simply annoying, or whether a film is a successful adaptation of a play or a novel. Whereas some of these disagreements might invoke categories, clearly not all of them need to invoke categories. But remember that Carroll is not committed to explaining every kind of evaluative disagreement about film. Nevertheless, it seems he must explain when it is sensible to compare films from different categories, according to their categories. Carroll suggests that this is sometimes a matter of comparing how films rank in their respective categories.[158] Other times, we may be engaged in a much broader kind of criticism whereby we compare films according to the cultural importance of the different categorical aims that they meet.[159] However, Carroll insists that it will not always make sense to compare very different films, perhaps because the aims of the categories to which they belong are of equal or unknown value.[160]

Whereas Carroll is careful to specify the limits of his account, he is firmly committed to the idea that categorical evaluation is a central, perhaps the central, kind of film evaluation. This may strike you as questionable, however, since it is often the case that when we say that a film is a good film of its kind, we imply that it is not very good on some broader scale. But what might this broader scale be? Perhaps it is a general artistic scale, as when we assess the expressiveness or composition of a film, or when we assess a film in terms of an important element that it shares with another art form, like the actors' performances. Alternatively, perhaps the broader scale of evaluation is a scale for film *per se*, as an art form. *Citizen Kane* (1941) has been called a 'supremely cinematic' film for the way it exploits what the film medium can and cannot show us directly. The film appears to make plain everything that happens in Kane's life and yet all it gives us are surface appearances, since Kane's inner life is left up to the viewers' imagination. The film is rich with interpretive possibilities and all because it exploits an apparent limitation of the medium as a visual record.[161] This is just one example, however, and it remains to be seen whether every film can be judged, not just as a certain kind of film, but just as a film.

Victor Perkins' *Film as Film: Understanding and Judging Movies*, as its title suggests, is concerned with just this question. This puts Perkins in the minority of film scholars who have looked beyond interpretation to criticism and the role of criticism in our enjoyment of films. With a focus on narrative fiction films, Perkins attempts to derive general evaluative criteria from an understanding of the formal possibilities inherent in the film medium. A film contains many elements and the key is to bring those elements into 'significant relationship' so as to create a unity which conveys the film-maker's vision. This is not easy to do because the medium pulls in opposite directions, both towards 'credibility' or realism and towards 'significance' or expression and communication. There is always a threat of 'collapse,' either the loss of illusion in the pursuit of expression or the loss of significance in the pursuit of realism.[162] The way in which a film avoids such a collapse, 'absorbs its tensions',[163] and achieves unity is by constraining expression with realism. The fewer 'one-function elements' a film has – in other words, the fewer elements it has which serve only to establish either credibility or significance – the better that film is.

To illustrate this point, Perkins compares a scene in *Rope* (1948) with a scene in *The Loudest Whisper* (1961).[164] Both scenes use the device of the 'controlled viewpoint' to create suspense. However, Perkins thinks that the former case involves a superior use of the expressive device which is less contrived because the device is motivated realistically.

In the scene from *Rope*, our view is restricted seemingly just by the parameters of the depicted apartment with which we are already familiar. In other words, suspense is generated by a restriction within the fictional world of the film. In the scene from *The Loudest Whisper*, on the other hand, we are suddenly prevented from hearing a crucial part of the ensuing conversation by the camera moving, in a cut, behind a glass partition. There is no reason within the story for our suddenly being cut off from the conversation – it is not as if the glass partition actually slides across our view, in the fiction, as we listen to the conversation. Instead, the suddenness and apparent arbitrariness of the change in camera position draws attention to itself as a device for creating suspense that breaks with the realism of the scene.

Perkins's measure for cinematic achievement is a kind of unity to be achieved through realistically motivated stylization. Thus the question we need to consider is whether this is really a measure for film as film rather than just a particular kind of film. In considering this question, it is significant that the kinds of films which are of the highest quality on Perkins's measure are Hollywood films from the late 1940s to the early 1960s. This suggests that Perkins's measure is appropriate to his examples just because it reflects the aims of the relevant tradition of filmmaking. Films in other traditions – for example, the tradition of modernism – that do not aim at realistic stylization are going to be judged poorly on Perkins's account. But it is clearly not the case that all modernist films are bad. To be fair to Perkins, however, despite the way the title of his book implies that he is interested in how we evaluate any kind of film just as film, he belatedly admits that he has 'deliberately restricted the field of this inquiry in order to examine sources of value within a particular form'.[165] This suggests that Perkins might just be doing the kind of evaluation that Carroll describes – identifying realistic stylization as a central aim of the category of classical Hollywood films and then assessing particular films according to the standards of that category.

Whether there can be a single evaluative standard for film as film remains an open question. Carroll is skeptical of this possibility, since attempts to identify such a standard often reflect a bias towards certain stylistic tendencies in the history of film. Nevertheless, the fact remains that film evaluation operates on multiple levels: When we evaluate films by category, the kinds of category we invoke vary in their breadth – from, say, *film noir* to melodrama to narrative fiction. But we can also praise a film for being 'pure cinema,' or even great art, which may involve an appeal to the place occupied by that film in the culture at large and the role it has played in people's lives.

CONCLUSIONS

Here is what we have covered in this chapter:

1. Bordwell's constructivist account of story comprehension, including his account of the actively inferential process of perceiving the images and sounds that make up the film, and his account of the imaginative process by which we follow a film's story and navigate the story-world.
2. Bordwell's analysis, if not his defence of, academic interpretation as a self-justifying and replicative practice.
3. The objection that Bordwell's constructivism does not support the claim that a film's meaning is made by the viewer.
4. Wilson's argument for a different kind of interpretation than the one Bordwell describes, a kind of explanatory interpretation not reserved for specialist critics.
5. Carroll's account of objective categorical film evaluation.
6. Perkins' criteria for judging 'film as film' which turn out to be criteria for judging one kind of film as that kind of film.

In this chapter we have learnt that the narrative film viewer is a thinking viewer, both during and after the viewing experience. This is not to say that the film viewer is cold, calculating, or distant. As we have seen, much of the viewer's cognitive activity is uncalculated just because it is unconscious and automatic. And, as we shall see in the next chapter, there are a great many ways in which a viewer can respond with feeling to a film. These responses often rely on our understanding of the film and may, in turn, influence how we interpret and evaluate it. Thus the division set up by this chapter and the next between the thinking and the feeling viewer is an artificial one simply for the purposes of analysis. The film viewer is in fact both thinking and feeling, and thinking may be a component of her feelings just as feeling may influence her thinking.

To return to the details of this chapter, Bordwell is surely right that comprehension is a complex constructive process even if that does not mean it is entirely up to the viewer what a film literally means. Similarly, if we take Bordwell to be providing a critical exposé of the current state of interpretation, we can reconcile his account with the possibility of other kinds of interpretation, including the explanatory kind described by Wilson. Whereas an ordinary viewer may be unlikely to attempt a psychoanalytic, auteurist, or otherwise theoretically laden 'reading' of a film, he is highly likely, especially when confronted by a particularly complex film, to engage in the interpretive process of reflective integration required to make the most sense of the film's narrative.

When it comes to evaluation, Carroll and Perkins have given us a lot to think about, particularly in relation to the remarkably varied and numerous criteria by which we judge different films. There is clearly a great deal of work still to be done on the rational foundations of film evaluation. At this stage, we must commend the film scholars who have begun this work. By breaking away from the mainstream of academic interpretation, they are able to reflect on the fact that, when it comes to film, everyone's a critic.

CHAPTER 7

THE FEELING FILM VIEWER

The ways in which we respond with feeling to films are rich and varied – arguably as rich and varied as the ways we respond in real life. We may pity the plight of the doomed heroine or feel tremendous anxiety as the shark approaches the unsuspecting swimmer, perhaps resisting the temptation to yell at the screen, 'Get out of the water!' We may automatically jump in our seats at a sudden explosion or recoil from the sight of a gruesome crime scene. We may feel indignant, sad, joyful, excited, apprehensive, dejected, frustrated, hopeful or jubilant, either along with the characters, on the behalf of the characters, or about some turn of events in the story. And lastly, we may be left feeling a certain a way by the film as a whole – perhaps vaguely anxious, buoyed up, exhilarated or sweetly melancholic.

All of these responses involve 'affect' or feeling, even if we do not consider all of them to involve emotions. You might not think that being startled by a sudden explosion counts as an emotion, since it is an automatic reflex response. Alternatively, you might not think that the anxious or melancholic mood that a film puts you in counts as an emotion because it is an amorphous state without an object – I am not anxious or melancholic about anything in particular. The distinction between emotions and other kinds of feeling is in fact contested even though philosophers have traditionally focused on a narrow class of emotions. For our purposes, it is important to recognize that such a distinction is often made even if, in the end, it may not be essential to uphold it.

Broadly speaking, an emotional response can be understood as a response to an event of significance to the subject involving bodily changes and typically characteristic motivating behaviour. Given the importance of emotions for the quality and meaning of life, it is not surprising that most of the great classical philosophers from Aristotle to Descartes to Hume have something to say about the nature of emotion. What is surprising, however, is that in the twentieth century, philosophers stopped paying attention to emotions. And it is only quite recently, partly in response to work in psychology, neurology, and evolutionary biology, that the philosophy of emotion has become a respectable field of study. Until even more recently, this field was dominated by a particular kind of theory that 1) only applies to the typical instances of paradigmatic emotions – for example, fear, anger and joy – but not to atypical instances of these emotions or to other kinds of feeling like moods and reflex responses; and, 2) distinguishes between different emotions by the cognitions they involve. Most commonly, the kind of cognition that an emotion is thought to involve is a belief or evaluation. Thus you can't be angry with someone unless you believe that she has slighted you; you can't be afraid of something unless you believe that it represents a threat. Even though both anger and fear are felt, bodily responses, what makes them anger and fear respectively, and not some other emotion, is the kind of belief they involve.

As we shall see, the assumption that every emotion involves a belief has led to some difficulties in accounting for our emotional responses to works of fiction, including fiction films. Recently, however, philosophers have begun to question whether a belief is absolutely required for having an emotion. This is partly a result of recognizing various situations in which emotions persist without the requisite belief – for example, when someone is afraid of flying despite knowing that it is safe. In response to the complexity of real-life cases, alternatives to the belief-theory have emerged. One alternative is to claim that emotions still necessarily involve a cognition but not a belief. Given the way that emotions focus our attention on those aspects of our situation which are most significant for us, this kind of theory suggests that the cognitive element of emotions is something like a perception, a construal or a way of seeing.[166] Another alternative is to claim that an emotion does not necessarily involve any kind of cognition. The crucial focus that an emotion provides is achieved by bodily means, and though emotions are influenced by cognition, they can be characterized in terms of their unique neurophysiological profiles.[167] This suggests that all felt responses could be emotions. While there are compelling arguments for both alternatives, as well as for the original belief-theory, we will not be defending a particular theory of emotion in this chapter. For our purposes, we need only take note of a growing philosophical appreciation of the complexity and heterogeneity of felt experience.

In the first two of the following three sections, we will be dealing almost exclusively with those feelings traditionally thought to be emotions because they take an object and involve cognition. Both of these sections deal with our emotional responses to characters or the narrative content of the film more generally. The first section examines two puzzles about our emotional responses to fictions. The second section examines one of the primary ways in which we engage with characters which is empathetic identification. Once we reach the third section, our perspective broadens to include the full range of feelings elicited, not just by what the film is about, but by the film itself in its stylistic and technical aspects. In this way, we will begin to see the remarkable extent to which film is a matter of feeling.

MAKING SENSE OF OUR FEELINGS FOR (FILM) FICTIONS

Since most of the films that we watch are works of narrative fiction, our analysis of film engagement cannot proceed without facing an apparent paradox concerning the intelligibility of having emotional responses to fictions. Fortunately for us, there is already an extensive literature on the so-called paradox of fiction. Since films are not the only kind of fiction, this paradox does not pertain exclusively to film. But if we wish to examine the ways in which various film structures support our felt engagement, we first need to make sure that we understand the nature of our engagement. After all, if it turns out that we cannot in fact respond with genuine feeling or emotion to fiction in general, we cannot proceed to an analysis of the ways in which fiction film in particular supports feeling.

A paradox is a piece of reasoning that appears perfectly sound but nevertheless leads to a false conclusion. To solve a paradox, you must show that the reasoning it involves, despite appearances to the contrary, really is unsound. This does not make the paradox disappear, since there is still a piece of reasoning that appears to be sound when it is not. But in solving the paradox, you show that the appearance of soundness is merely that – an appearance. You may even go on to explain why the piece of reasoning under consideration has this appearance, thereby preparing others not to be fooled. Alternatively, you could simply accept the contradiction implied by the paradox and learn to live with it. Both of these approaches have been taken to the paradox of fiction.

The Paradox of Fiction

The paradox of fiction is often expressed in terms of three propositions, all of which seem true even though they cannot all be true without yielding a contradiction.

1. We only respond emotionally to what we believe to be real.
2. We do not believe that fiction is real.

From these two premises, it seems to follow that we do not respond emotionally to fiction. And yet it seems that

3. we respond emotionally to fiction all the time.[168]

Those who are committed to solving the paradox of fiction aim to show that one of these propositions is false. Others, though admittedly a minority, have accepted the paradox and concluded that our responses to fiction are simply irrational.[169] If, however, you find it implausible to think that we lose all sense of reason as soon as we become engaged with fiction, it is worth pursuing a solution to the paradox.

The debate about the paradox of fiction has evolved to the point where a significant number of those involved agree that the best route to a solution involves a denial of the first proposition – that we only respond emotionally to what we believe to be real. Before embarking on this route, however, we need at least to consider solutions that involve denying either the second or the third proposition.

In order to solve the paradox by denying the second proposition, one has to give an account of how, in the course of engaging with fiction, one's belief that the characters and events of the fiction are not real is temporarily suspended.[170] It turns out that giving such an account is difficult to do. In real life, we might suspend a particular belief before discarding it completely in the face of new evidence that challenges the belief in question. But this does not seem to be what's going on when we engage with fiction, since there is no new evidence to challenge my belief that, for example, the zombies depicted on screen are not real. You might reply, however, that the fiction itself provides the evidence – the incredibly life-like images of the zombies compel me at least to suspend my disbelief, if not quite adopt a new belief, in real-life zombies. But there is a problem with this reply. If it is the fiction that supplies the evidence that challenges my belief, then I must have already suspended my belief that the fiction is not real in order to have the evidence I need for suspending my belief that the fiction is not real. If I have already suspended my belief in order to treat the fiction as evidence, it cannot be the fiction that provides evidence supporting a suspension of belief.

Even if it were possible to suspend our belief that the fiction is not real, the way that we experience fictions suggests that this is not what's going on. If I no longer believed that the vicious zombies on screen were fictional, I would surely not remain seated in the cinema for long. Presumably, upon discovering that there are killer-zombies on the loose, I would alert the authorities and take measures to protect myself and my loved ones. But I do not do this. In other words, I do not act as though I have suspended my belief that the fiction is not real. Moreover, it is not just that I stay seated in the cinema, but I seem to be enjoying myself as I watch the zombies approaching on screen. I am able to appreciate the vivid depiction of an army of zombies surging forward with arms outstretched, the use of special effects or highly emotive music, the importance of this scene for the narrative, and so on. Surely, if I had suspended my belief that the zombies are fictional, I would be too frightened to appreciate the film in this way.

So much for solving the paradox by denying the second proposition. What about a solution that involves denying the third proposition – that we respond emotionally to fictions? Philosophers who attempt a solution of this kind do not deny that we respond to fiction at all. Rather, they deny that our responses consist in genuine emotions.[171] Instead our responses to fiction consist in fictional, make-believe, or pretend emotions. These responses may have a genuine feel to them – while watching the zombies approach, I feel my heart pounding and my hands turning clammy as I grip the arms of my seat. But assuming that our responses cannot be reduced to brute feeling, insofar as they only involve beliefs about what is fictionally the case, they cannot be real emotions.

This kind of solution immediately raises some questions: What exactly is a fictional emotional response? How can a real person have a fictional response? And if none of the components of the response are fictional, why is the response itself still only fictional? A belief about what is fictionally the case is still a genuine belief, after all. And the feelings involved in my response are most certainly genuine insofar as I am experiencing changes in my body that can be objectively measured. The only component of my response that is fictional is its object, what my response is directed towards – for example, the zombies on screen. And while the status of an emotion's object is important for determining the appropriateness of the response, it does not determine that the response is a genuine emotion. If my fear is directed at a kitten, we might want to say that my fear is inappropriate. But it is still fear. Moreover, some of our emotions seem not to take an object at all – for example, when I feel angry but do not know what about – and yet they are no less real for that.

Solutions to the paradox of fiction that involve denying the third proposition thus leave us wondering why beliefs about what is fictionally the case – that is, that there are zombies on the loose – cannot inspire genuine emotions. This brings us to the third kind of solution to the paradox of fiction which denies the first proposition – that we only respond emotionally to what we believe to be real. The most common form of this solution consists in a denial, not just of the necessity of a belief in the reality of the object of our emotion, but of the necessity of any kind of belief for a genuine emotional response. In other words, this solution engages with the current debate in the philosophy of emotion about what kind of cognition, if any, is essential to emotion.

The philosopher who wishes to solve the paradox of fiction by denying the first proposition has two options: She can accept that emotions always involve cognition but deny that emotions always involve beliefs. Then she can suggest that emotions involve another kind of cognition like a thought or a perception which, unlike belief, is supported by fiction. Alternatively, she can refuse to accept that emotions always involve any kind of cognition. Then she can suggest that film media are ideally suited for the spontaneous excitation of emotion or feeling without any cognitive processing. Films are particularly good at exploiting our phobias, for example, in an automatic, visual way – swinging aerial camerawork or the image of a writhing mass of snakes may be enough to trigger a viewer's vertigo or ophidiophobia, respectively. A potential difficulty with this second option, however, is that those felt responses to films that are automatic and visceral tend to be triggered by stylistic and technical means rather than by the film's content. But the paradox of fiction concerns just those responses we have to characters and events which are part of content. For this reason, we will leave aside the possibility of emotions without cognition until we reach our discussion, in the final section, of the general emotional appeal of a film.

Several philosophers who take the first option claim that a fiction prescribes particular imaginings or thoughts about its content and these imaginings or thoughts in themselves inspire an emotional response.[172]

In real life, we may shudder at the thought of something horrible or amuse ourselves with whimsical imaginings. This, some claim, is all that is going on with fiction but in a more systematic way. When I am shown a zombie on the film screen in all its horrible detail, I think about or imagine just what I am shown. In other words, the depiction of the zombie constitutes the content of my thought or imagining. But I can think about or imagine the depicted zombie as a combination of just those properties specified in the depiction without believing in the zombie. I can think about a creature that looks human except for its dead eyes and pallid skin, its trance-like lumbering movements, its unstoppable drive to kill, and so on, for all the features of the zombie that I recognize, independently from each other, from real life. Moreover, it is very easy for me to do this given the vivid moving image of the zombie projected right in front of me.

One objection to this account is that it fails to preserve the intuition that the zombie itself is the object of my fear.[173] If you ask me what I'm afraid of, I'll say the zombie. I certainly won't say that I'm afraid of my thought about the zombie. However, this objection fails to recognize that there are different kinds of object that an emotion can take, and that the cause and object of an emotion need not be the same. Thus while I am frightened *by* the thought of the zombie – the thought causes my emotion, I am frightened *of* the content of the thought; namely, the zombie itself. My thinking about the zombie is what makes me afraid but it is what I am thinking about that is the target of my fear.

Another objection to the thought or imagining account is that it is limited in scope. Even if it is the case that I could be frightened by the thought of the zombie, it is also possible that I am frightened simply by what I see on screen, without thinking much about it at all. Just the look of the zombie – those dead eyes and that cadaverous complexion, the reaching arms and unnatural movements – is enough to scare me. My response is more immediate than what one would expect if it involved a lot of thought. Moreover, the possibility of this kind of responsive immediacy is supported by recent experiments in neurophysiology. These experiments show that the emotional processing of perceptual data can occur independently of cognitive processing because there is a direct route from the perceptual apparatus to those parts of the brain that are crucial in generating emotion. Perhaps, then, the most promising solution to the paradox of fiction involves pointing to a range of emotional triggers – thoughts, imaginings, and perceptions – that can substitute for the belief that the fiction is real.

The Paradox of Horror

Once we expand our understanding of emotions, it seems that the paradox of fiction is eminently solvable. Unfortunately, however, we are not yet free of complications surrounding our felt engagement with fiction film. Even if we can respond with genuine emotions to fiction, a further paradox emerges when those responses are negative and thus intrinsically unpleasant – emotions like fear, pity, anxiety, and sadness. In real life, these are the sorts of emotions that we do not want to have. But in the context of fiction, some people appear to seek them out and even enjoy them.

This paradox arises with the enjoyment of any negative emotion in the context of fiction. However, there are particular versions of the paradox for particular genres of fiction that are defined in terms of the kinds of response that they aim to evoke. The paradox of tragedy has a long and distinguished philosophical history: Aristotle and later Hume were both puzzled by the way that tragedy aims and often succeeds in creating an enjoyable experience of fear and pity. More recently, philosophers have turned to the paradox of horror, which will be our focus here. The reason for this focus is that by far the largest portion of horror fictions are films. Indeed, there seems to be something about film media which make them particularly well-suited both to the depiction of horror and to the evocation of the emotions of fear and disgust that define the genre.[174]

Just like the paradox of fiction, the paradox of horror can be expressed in terms of three propositions, all of which seem true but together yield a contradiction.

1. Negative emotions like fear and disgust are intrinsically unpleasant.
2. Horror fictions aim to evoke fear and disgust.
3. Some people enjoy horror fictions

If what it means for an emotion to be negative is just that it is experienced as unpleasant, and if this amounts to the same thing as our not enjoying the emotion, given that we cannot simultaneously enjoy and not enjoy the exact same thing, it seems to follow from these two premises that we cannot enjoy horror fictions, or at least not the emotive aspect of horror fictions. And yet, it certainly appears as though some people enjoy horror fictions, and what they enjoy about horror fictions is just that the fictions are frightening and disgusting.

One approach to solving the paradox involves claiming that what some of us enjoy about horror is not the fear and disgust evoked but something else – for example, the arousal and satisfaction of our curiosity about the impossible creatures we encounter on screen,[175] or the sense had at the end of a film that we have worked unpleasant emotions out of our system.[176] Perhaps one could also claim that we enjoy a particular component of fear and disgust – for example, the 'rush' we feel as our body releases a burst of adrenalin and our heart rate increases – but that this does not amount to enjoying the emotions themselves. Finally, one could claim that we enjoy a sense of our own courage or resolve in being able to face unpleasant emotions at least in the context of fiction.

The trouble with all the solutions of this kind, however, is that they essentially miss the point. There is only a paradox to solve in the first place if we grant that some of us enjoy fear and disgust. But this is precisely what solutions of this kind refuse to grant. The challenge is thus to explain how we can enjoy negative emotions given that they are negative and thus unpleasant. One way to meet this challenge is to argue that we can enjoy negative emotions because negative emotions are only contingently unpleasant. Some theorists claim that we can enjoy negative emotions when they are under our control – for example, when I can direct my attention away from the gory bits in a horror film.[177] Other theorists claim that we can enjoy negative emotions as long as they do not take an unpleasant object. Fear is only unpleasant in real life insofar as it is directed at something unpleasant – specifically something that constitutes a threat. When I fear a fictional monster on screen, I am not responding to a genuine threat and thus my fear need not be unpleasant.

There are various problems specific to each of these suggestions, but one problem they have in common is that in making negative emotions only contingently unpleasant, they seem to go against our understanding of negative emotions. If someone told you that the emotion he experienced on the death of his beloved great aunt was highly enjoyable, you would surely hesitate to call his emotion grief.[178] This suggests that the connection between the negativity and unpleasantness of an emotion is necessary rather than contingent. But now we are back at square one, facing once again the paradox of enjoying what, by definition, cannot be enjoyed.

There may still be a way out of this bind, however. Berys Gaut suggests that only in the typical case are negative emotions experienced as unpleasant.[179] This means that, necessarily typically, negative emotions are unpleasant. In the atypical case, however, this need not be so. Atypical cases are not limited to fiction but include cases like the enjoyment of extreme sports and roller coasters. But the experience of horror is the atypical case in which we are interested. In the atypical case, what makes a negative emotion still count as a negative emotion when it is experienced as pleasant is just the background of typical cases in which human beings experience the emotion as unpleasant. Just as what the masochist enjoys only counts as pain against a background of normal aversive reactions, so what the horror buff enjoys only counts as fear against a background of unpleasant experiences.

In his own careful and detailed presentation of the argument, Gaut spells out the various philosophical presuppositions that are required for this solution to work. If there is something about the way that Gaut's solution appeals to the typical case that doesn't seem quite right to you, the next step would be to examine closely the presuppositions that ground this appeal. Then again, you may still be inclined to think that there is no paradox needing to be solved in the first place. That is, you may suspect that it is never the case that what we enjoy about horror fictions is the fear and disgust that they evoke. Even when a horror buff complains that a particular horror film wasn't frightening enough to be enjoyable, this need not indicate that when the horror buff does enjoy a horror film, what she enjoys is being frightened (and disgusted). Perhaps instead, by complaining that a particular horror film wasn't frightening enough, the horror buff is signalling that the film failed to be convincing as a result of poor narrative structure, editing, or special effects. Moreover, the horror buff may describe a good horror film as frightening without being frightened herself. Probably she wouldn't be such a buff if she was being frightened all the time. Rather, when she describes a good horror film as frightening it is because she recognizes that, in general, a good horror film can frighten people even though the ones who are frightened tend not to enjoy the film.

Before leaving the paradox of horror, it is worth noting one other way in which our fear of horror is disputed. Is our fear, fear for the endangered characters or fear for ourselves? Am I frightened of the zombies, along with the characters, or am I frightened for the characters, whether or not they're frightened themselves, because they are endangered by the zombies? Some theorists deny that it ever makes sense to fear for ourselves in response to fiction because we cannot actually be threatened by something that is only fictionally dangerous. And yet, we often talk as though we're afraid of the same horrors as the characters. Perhaps what feels like genuine fear in these cases is really only pretend or imagined fear. But perhaps not. In the next section, we will consider how we may come to share genuine emotions like fear with characters through an act of identification.

IDENTIFICATION AND EMPATHY

When ordinary film-goers talk about their experience with a particular character – usually a protagonist – in a film, it is quite common to hear remarks of the following kind:

'I could really identify with her';
'I think the scene moved me so deeply because I identified with him'; and,
'There was nothing about her with which I could identify'.

It is highly likely that the first two remarks are part of a positive evaluation, and the third remark part of a negative evaluation, not just of the way a particular character is developed, but of the film as a whole. Indeed, remarking on whether or not a central character with whom we are clearly meant to identify is one with whom we really can identify may make the difference between a good and a bad film – or a highly engaging and a not-so-engaging film. Given this, and our everyday ways of talking about whether or not we like a film, identification seems to be a phenomenon that we cannot ignore in this chapter.

But what exactly *is* identification and why is it so important? It is this question that will concern us here. In what follows, we will link what we ordinarily mean when we talk about identification with the various ways in which theorists have handled the notion. First we will consider what psychoanalytic film theorists have to say, then what cognitive film theorists and philosophers have to say, about identification. Ultimately, we will conclude that identification is a valuable imaginative process that supports empathetic responses to characters.

This is not meant to suggest that identification represents the only way in which we engage with film characters. When we identify with a character we seem to share her emotional response – for example, when the zombies scare me almost as much as they do the film's protagonist. But as well, we can have responses to characters that are not shared with them – for example, when I pity a character that is in no way self-pitying. Such responses are usually described as sympathetic whereas responses involving identification are usually described as empathetic. Even though we will also explore this distinction in what follows, our focus will remain on identification.[180] This is because identification is perhaps the most mysterious and misunderstood, but also the most powerfully intimate, aspect of our felt engagement with film characters.

Psychoanalytic Identification

One of the defining characteristics of 'psycho-semiotic' film theory is its use of psychoanalytic theory – particularly of the Lacanian variety – to understand our experience of film. Given this, it is no surprise that a standard notion of cinematic identification in film theory is modelled on a particular subconscious phenomenon that psychoanalytic theorists take to be central to our psychosexual development. In fact, the reason that psychoanalytic film theorists call cinematic identification, 'identification,' is just because this is what Lacan calls the analogous developmental phenomenon.

According to Lacan, one of the most significant stages in our psychosexual development is the so-called mirror stage. This is the stage we enter at around eighteen months of age when we develop a powerful sense of self by identifying with our own mirror images. Seeing our reflected selves for the first time entails recognizing ourselves as discrete individuals for the first time. This recognition is partly mistaken, however, because the infant assumes that his mirror-image self has the motor capacities that the infant himself has yet to develop but which match his current mental capacity. Thus Lacan implies that identification, whether with one's own image in infancy or with others later on, involves the projection of an 'ego ideal' such that one sees an enhanced version of oneself in the object of identification. In film, Lacanian theorists use this idea to explain the identification of viewers with the larger-than-life heroes portrayed on screen.

It is worth noting that this notion of hero identification in the psychoanalytic tradition has inspired a feminist critique of our engagement with mainstream film. In a highly influential article,[181] British film-maker, critic, and theorist, Laura Mulvey, claims that traditional movie heroes exhibit masculine traits and thus only male (or 'masculinized') viewers identify with them. In turn, this gives the male viewer a sense of control over the events of the story. Such control is crucial for counteracting the effect of the female screen icon, which, by demanding erotic contemplation, effectively stalls the narrative. In this way, the sense of empowerment derived from identification in general takes a particular and patriarchal form in the context of narrative film. Interestingly, Mulvey's critique, while provocative and revealing, does not question the psychoanalytic account of identification. Rather it assumes the truth of this account in order to claim that mainstream film serves patriarchal ends. Thus, for the sake of coming to a critical understanding of identification, we can turn our attention back to the psychoanalytic account itself.

According to Christian Metz, the most influential of the psychoanalytic film theorists, part of what explains why we watch films and how we make sense of them is that film reactivates infantile identification. The crucial similarity is what Metz calls, 'the play of presence and absence' – the simultaneous presence of an image and absence of the referent on the screen or in the mirror. It is because our infantile experience with the mirror and our experience with film are both experiences of the play of presence and absence that Metz thinks we can understand them in terms of the same subconscious process of identification.[182]

The pleasure of identification explains why we enjoy watching films. More importantly for Metz, however, the role that Lacan assigns identification in communication explains how we make sense of films. According to Lacan, any kind of communication – and social life in general – is impossible without the alternation of the subject position facilitated by identification. The fact that I have to identify with someone in order to understand what she is telling me suggests to Metz that I also have to identify with the source of telling (and showing) in a film in order to understand the film. The source of a film's telling and showing is, in a literal sense, the camera. Thus the fundamental role of identification in communication leads Metz to claim that identification with the camera is the primary form of identification in film. Identification with characters is secondary because the intelligibility of film in general does not depend on it. After all, there are intelligible films that do not have characters.

There is clearly much to be questioned in Metz's theory. Is the psychoanalytic account of identification even plausible and is Metz really justified in applying this account to film? Moreover, does the way in which Metz applies this account, assuming the account makes sense, really illuminate the cinematic experience? What does it mean, exactly, to identify with the camera? All these questions and more have been taken up by critics of the psychoanalytic approach to film. While it is crucial to do this, what is most important for our purposes is to consider whether the psychoanalytic account of film identification helps us make sense of the kinds of things we say about identification when we leave the cinema or turn off the television.

Whatever conclusion one reaches about the plausibility of the psycho-analytic account, the fact remains that this account does not seem to apply to the kind of identification we actually talk about. Personally, I have never heard anyone emerge from the cinema saying, 'gosh, I could really identify with the camera in that film!' Indeed, insofar as psycho-analytic identification is subconscious, we wouldn't be in a position to comment spontaneously on our having identified with the camera. Of course, if we were well-versed in psychoanalytic film theory, we might infer from our comprehension of the film that identification had occurred. But if this kind of inference grounded any remark about iden-tification, the evaluative weight of these remarks would be lost. When we say something about the way a film supports identification, we mean to single out that film – not just as one of many films which are intelli-gible, but as a good film among intelligible films. According to the psychoanalytic film theorist, primary identification occurs in every case of our understanding a film and thus doesn't seem to be something worth remarking on. The fact that we do remark on identification sug-gests that we need to look elsewhere for an explanation of the conscious phenomenon of character identification.[183]

So where might we look? The obvious place would be in another branch of film theory – cognitive film theory. Unfortunately, some cogni-tive film theorists and philosophers of film are so suspicious of the historical link between identification and psychoanalysis that they wish to abandon the notion altogether. The highly circumscribed and idiosyn-cratic use of the term 'identification' by psychoanalytic film theorists just highlights for them the instability and heterogeneity of the notion in general. Noël Carroll, for instance, gives us a sample list of all the differ-ent things we can mean by 'identification' with characters:

> ... that we like the protagonist; that we recognize the circumstances of the protagonist to be significantly like those we have found or find ourselves in; that we sympathize with the protagonist; that we are one in interest, or feeling, or principle, or all of these with the protagonist; that we see the action unfolding in the fiction from the protagonist's point of view; that we share the protagonist's values; that, for the duration of our intercourse with the fiction, we are under the illusion that each of us somehow regards herself to be the protagonist.[184]

If 'identification' is being used to cover all of these phenomena, *plus* the subconscious phenomenon that psychoanalytic film theorists are interested in, how useful can this term really be? This is only the first of Carroll's worries, however. He also argues that even if we can isolate a core meaning of the term, 'identification,' the phenomenon it refers to is not part – or not a significant part – of our cinematic experience. Carroll suggests that the core meaning of 'identification' concerns the viewer's duplication of a character's emotion through empathy but he denies that this regularly – perhaps ever – occurs. This is because, automatically, an actual person watching a film and a fictional character in the film stand in very different relations to the events of the story. For the character, those events are real and directly affect her fate. For the viewer, on the other hand, those events are fictional and the character's fate is part of a larger constructed whole. This means that even if the character and the viewer have the same kind of emotion, the viewer's response does not duplicate the character's because it takes a different object. So, for example, if both the viewer and the character experience fear, the viewer's fear is fear for the character whereas the character's fear is fear for himself. As well, the character's fear is fear of a personal threat whereas the viewer's fear is a fear of a threat to the character and may be mixed with other emotions that the character does not have like enjoyment or curiosity.

Carroll's objections deserve our attention and further ahead we will consider how to respond to them. First, however, we can use these objections to guide our analysis of identification. Carroll shows us that if we want to explain what we mean when we say things like, 'I could really identify with Erin Brockovitch,' or '. . . with Donnie Darko,' or '. . . with Atanarjuat the Fast Runner,' we will have to meet several requirements. We have to (1) locate the core meaning of the term 'identification'; (2) give a plausible account of this core meaning; and, (3) show that identification on this account is an important aspect of our engagement with film.

Imaginative Identification

In fact, the first of these requirements is easy to fulfil because we can agree with Carroll that the core sense of 'identification' has to do with emotional duplication or empathy. All of the philosophical accounts of identification that we will draw on in this chapter link identification and empathy. On its own, the idea of empathy as emotional duplication sounds mysterious and unlikely. It is therefore unsurprising that Carroll would approach the whole question of identification with such scepticism. But with the right account of how empathy comes about, we can begin to appreciate the short-sightedness of Carroll's skepticism. Indeed, the rest of this section will show that the most substantial work to be done in giving a philosophical account of identification is in explaining the process behind empathy rather than empathy itself.

Among those cognitive film theorists and philosophers who refuse to dismiss the notion, Richard Wollheim's account of central imagining is regarded as the best resource for understanding character identification.[185] According to Wollheim, there are two varieties of representational imagining that can occur in any mode of perception – central and acentral imagining. In the visual mode, both central and acentral imagining involve, not just imagining that you see something, but imagining seeing – or visualizing – it. The difference between central and acentral imagining is that central imagining involves imagining seeing from a certain point of view, whereas acentral imagining involves imagining seeing from no particular point of view – in other words, without the filter of a particular person's perspective. Thus, to use Wollheim's own example, suppose that while reading Gibbon's history of the Roman Empire you conjure up an image of the celebrated entry of Sultan Mahomet II into Constantinople. Either you can visualize the event acentrally – 'as stretched out, frieze-like, the far side of the invisible chasm of history'[186] – or you can visualize it centrally, from the perspective of one of the participants – say, the Sultan himself. In the latter case, you are representing, for your own inner viewing pleasure, what the Sultan saw of the event. As long as you know enough about the Sultan (say, from Gibbon's description) to infer how he would have experienced the event, you can centrally imagine the Sultan's (visual) experience as though it were your own.

Central imagining is thus imagining what another person is going through *as though* you are the other person. It is not that you are deluded about really being this person. It is just that, in imagination, you share the other person's experience. This helps us see why some philosophers and film theorists use Wollheim's account of central imagining to explain cinematic identification. Skeptics who argue that identification is not part of film engagement often take 'identification' literally and then point to difficulties with the idea of imagining oneself identical with another.[187] Wollheim's account of central imagining lines up more closely with how we actually use the term 'identification'. By 'identification' we mean, not 'melding' with a character, but 'living' with her: sharing her cares and coming to understand her in a particularly intimate way.[188] There are surely many things about another that we could only begin to understand by finding out, through an act of imagination, what it is like to have his point of view. In turn, the understanding that naturally accompanies central imagining breeds care and concern.

Wollheim's account of central imagining provides the beginnings of an explanation of the imaginative route to empathy. Having completed his description of central imagining, Wollheim sums up by listing what he takes to be the three essential features of this phenomenon: point of view, plenitude, and cogency.[189] The first of these features has already been mentioned. But what of plenitude and cogency? Plenitude describes the way that my imaginative project tends to develop a life of its own so that, by imagining doing and saying what the protagonist does and says, I naturally end up imagining thinking and feeling as she most likely thinks and feels. In turn, the cogency of central imaginings depends on their plenitude and describes their special psychic power: By imagining thinking and feeling as the character thinks and feels, there is every chance that I will be left in the condition – cognitive, conative, but particularly affective – in which the imagined mental states, were I actually to have them, would leave me. This suggests that a particular kind of emotional state could follow from identification. More is needed, however, to confirm that this state is empathetic.

In his 'aspectual' account of empathetic identification, Berys Gaut provides this confirmation.[190] Gaut's account might be seen to follow from an explication of Wollheim's idea that central imagining involves imagining different components of another's experience – percepts, actions, thoughts, desires and feelings. Given the limits on just how much we can imagine in one instance, Gaut argues that identification is necessarily partial and can take several forms. Insofar as I can imagine perceiving, believing, desiring, or feeling what another perceives, believes, desires, or feels, I can achieve perceptual, epistemic, motivational, or affective identification. The variety of forms that identification can take is limited only by the variety of aspects of another's experience I can imagine having. Moreover, different forms of identification can combine simultaneously as well as foster one another.

Since some of our beliefs are perceptual, just by imagining perceiving what a character perceives, I achieve a degree of epistemic identification. As well, however, just like actual perceiving supports beliefs that are not just perceptual, so imagined perceiving supports imagined beliefs that are not just perceptual. Once I have imagined seeing and believing what the character sees and believes, and given that the character's desires and emotions are based, in large part, on what he sees and believes, there is then every chance that I will also achieve some degree of motivational and affective identification with the character. But, as we know from Wollheim's emphasis on the feature of cogency, the course of my engagement need not end here. Gaut argues from common experience that imagining feeling what the character feels can foster actually feeling what the character feels. Any emotion can be experienced empathetically just as long as it is someone else's in the first place.

Empathetic Identification

If empathy fundamentally involves imaginative identification, then we can appreciate that not every incidence of concurring emotion is going to count as empathy. I might happen to react in the same way to the same event as someone else – as is often the case with fans at a sporting event or members of a cinema audience. But this does not mean I am empathizing with the other person. For empathy to occur, I have to respond in the same way as another *because* she responds that way.[191] There is thus a special relationship between my response and the response of whomever it is with whom I empathize. Fortunately, we already have the resources to explain this special relationship; namely, an account of imaginative identification.

Insofar as empathy is not just the coincidence but the sharing of emotion, it requires the imaginative adoption of the grounds of another's emotion, or the particular experience and perspective which gives rise to just that emotion. For me to share Maria's fear of the bear, it is not that I have to be in the presence of the bear and judging the bear to be dangerous. Then, presumably, I would be having my own fear but not sharing Maria's. Rather, I need to imaginatively adopt Maria's experience of the situation with the bear – *her* belief about the dangerousness of the bear; *her* desire to run from the bear, and, indeed, *her* feelings about the bear. If I can imaginatively adopt Maria's perspective in this way, and if affective identification tends to foster empathy, then the relationship between my response and Maria's would seem to be one of identity.

This brings us to another important distinction: The distinction between empathy and sympathy. One handy way of explicating the distinction is to say that empathy is feeling with a character and sympathy is feeling for a character. Thus I can have the same kind of emotion both empathetically and sympathetically – I can be happy with you and for you. There is more to the distinction than this, however. A number of theorists have pointed out that empathy is a success term in a way that sympathy is not.[192] An empathetic emotion can only really be empathetic if the person with whom one empathizes is really feeling that emotion – if you take someone to be feeling fear and thus feel fear yourself when, in fact, the other person is not feeling fear, then you have not succeeded in empathizing with him. In contrast, whether or not I am mistaken about what the other is feeling – and even if the other is not feeling anything – I can have a sympathetic response to him. A sympathetic response does not depend on the other's actual emotion but on a concerned judgment of her situation. You fear for someone because you judge him to be in danger and this concerns you whether or not the person has realized the danger himself.

Thus even though the terms, 'empathy' and 'sympathy' are often used loosely and interchangeably in everyday life, there is still a substantial distinction to be made between two categories of response to other, real and fictional, people. In fact, however, the tendency to use the terms rather loosely may be taken to reflect the way empathy can foster sympathy and sympathy can foster empathy. Gaut makes the point that, insofar as most people are concerned for themselves, by empathizing with someone you may come to share her concern.[193] And as we have seen, sympathy depends on a concerned judgment of another. In addition, Gaut notes that by sympathizing with someone you may align yourself emotionally with him to the point that you end up empathizing as well.[194]

Now that we have an account of imaginative and empathetic identification, we can respond to Noël Carroll's objections to the possibility or likelihood of this phenomenon. Recall that Carroll argues that identification cannot occur because emotional duplication cannot occur. And emotional duplication cannot occur because the viewer and the character stand in such different relations to the events of the story that their emotions, even when they are of the same kind, are going to have a different scope and direction.

What can we say to Carroll? First of all, we can say that his objections have failed to engage with or even acknowledge the imaginative component of identification. Whatever Carroll has to say about emotional duplication or empathy does not touch the plausibility of central imagining. As a result of this oversight, however, Carroll's objections to empathy itself are undermined. Once you take into account the imaginative activity behind empathy, emotional duplication suddenly makes sense. It is not, in fact, the case that the viewer's and the character's responses have a different direction and scope. When the viewer centrally imagines experiencing the story events as the character does, then the viewer's response is *just like* the character's – it is based on the same experience imaginatively realized.[195]

Of course, this response assumes that the emotional duplication that Carroll is objecting to is the kind based on imaginative identification. In the literature on empathy and identification, there are at least two other kinds of account of emotional duplication. The first deals with what is called affective mimicry. The second deals with a different imaginative process than the one described above called simulation, which is thought to support shared responses. Affective mimicry involves an automatic response to the registering of emotional expression in others. Thus when I see a close-up on screen of someone crying, I may involuntarily and unconsciously adopt a similar expression – my facial muscles tense in a certain way, my mouth turns downward, and so on. My expression then has a 'feedback' effect: Suddenly I am feeling how I look. In other words, I end up mimicking in feeling what I have subconsciously taken to be expressed by the other person.[196] For this to occur, however, we don't need to know why the other person is feeling what they express. But many philosophers think that a feeling is not a full-fledged emotion unless it is felt for a reason. In other words, many philosophers think that emotions involve a feeling that is caused by having a certain conception of, or thought or belief about, one's situation. Thus, although my mimicked state might feel like sadness, it is not sadness proper. Moreover, if this is right, we cannot really refer to affective mimicry as full emotional duplication or empathy.

Simulation is a process of imaginatively 'trying on' another's beliefs, desires, or attitudes in order either to reach an understanding of her current behaviour or to predict her future behaviour. There are close parallels between this kind of account and our account of central imagining, since, on both accounts, the imaginative adoption of another's perspective leads to emotional engagement. Unfortunately, however, recent work in the philosophy of mind has cast significant doubt on whether simulation is really how we come to understand other people. Furthermore, whether in the context of fiction or real life, simulation only results in imagined and not real emotions,[197] and no explanation is given of the possibility of moving from imagined feeling to the actual feelings involved in an empathetic response.

If imaginative identification is the sole or primary route to empathetic engagement with film characters, then its significance is secured. However, for some theorists, there is a further reason for attempting to resolve all the complications surrounding the notion of identification, and this is that an account can be given of the unique way that identification contributes to our understanding of characters and our own emotional responses to characters. This is because imaginative identification allows us to adopt someone else's perspective and respond from that perspective, thereby giving us some reflective distance on our own perspective and typical responses.[198] Although we do not have the space to fully explore this idea here, it is important to mention because it may help explain the observation we made at the beginning of the section – that the possibility of identification can make the difference between a good and a bad film.

Not all good narrative films support identification, however. Indeed, some narrative films fail to support any kind of emotional engagement with characters. This may be because a film has no characters – as in the case of *Koyaanisqatsi* (1983). It may also be because the characters a film does have are inaccessible and dispassionate – as in the case of *The Man Who Wasn't There* (2001). The fact that such films can nevertheless be intensely moving suggests that there is more to our felt engagement with film than our engagement with film characters.

FILM FORM AND FEELING

It is not surprising that so far most of the work on our felt engagement with film has focused on our responses to film characters and narrative content more generally. After all, Hollywood-style films tend to privilege character and narrative development. It is usually the actions of characters that drive the plot forward, and our expectations about whether the characters will meet their goals determine how we make sense of the plot. These expectations also govern our appreciation of the filmmakers' stylistic choices in terms of narrative significance. Nevertheless, while the focus on characters and content may be understandable, it is still unduly limiting. We not only respond to content but also to form or style, and sometimes we respond to form regardless of content.

A film's camerawork, lighting, editing, *mise en scène*, music, and sound effects can be used to trigger emotional responses that, in turn, reinforce the significance of narrative events. But even when what is depicted has little or no narrative significance, the way it is depicted can have an emotional effect – for example, in the way that rapidly changing light gradients can trigger an immediate response of fear. In general terms, however, responses to form alone still support responses to content because the consistency of our responses to characters can best be explained in terms of the emotive function of form.

This brings us to what we shall call the consistency puzzle: How does a film reliably elicit the same responses from a diverse audience? In real life we do not expect this to happen. If, for example, a couple is arguing on a street corner, passers-by are likely to respond in any number of ways. Some of them may be annoyed at the disturbance; others may feel embarrassed for the couple; still others may feel sorry for one or both members of the couple. Each kind of response rests on a different interpretation of the event, influenced by the personality, background assumptions and life experience of the person passing by.[199] But imagine that you are watching the couple argue, not on the street corner but in a film. Now it seems that there is only one right way for everyone to respond and this is in fact the way that most of us do respond. How do we explain this difference?

One way to solve the consistency puzzle involves an analysis of the way that films – particularly through their formal features – exploit or appropriate the function of emotions. Noël Carroll argues that in real life, emotional responses function to focus our attention on or make salient those aspects of our situation that are significant for our goals and interests. Films can take over this focusing function and thereby secure our attention in just the way required for a particular intended emotional response.[200] Carroll is not alone in claiming that emotions have a focusing function. This claim is also made by theorists who emphasize the analogy between emotion and perception,[201] and theorists who think of emotion as a physiological alerting mechanism.[202] Moreover, from first reflection on our own emotional experience, it is not hard to see why this claim is commonly made. When I am afraid, I am automatically focused on what is frightening and therefore threatening about my situation. When I am angry, I am automatically focused on what is angering and therefore unjust about my situation. This suggests to Carroll that if a film can establish the right focus for a particular emotion, then most viewers will respond with just that emotion.

In order to illustrate Carroll's claim, let's return to the example of the arguing couple. In the film version of the argument, let's say we are meant to feel indignant on behalf of one member of the couple.

The film-makers will then have set things up so that our attention is drawn to the character's decency and how she is being unfairly treated. How the film-makers do this depends on a myriad choices about how to tell the story, who to choose for the role – perhaps an actor with an air of vulnerability or one who tends to play decent and sympathetic characters, how to construct the dialogue, and how to shoot and edit the scene of the argument so as to favour one character – perhaps through the use of close-ups, gentler lighting, and musical punctuation. Whereas in real life, passers-by respond according to their own interpretations of the situation, in the film, viewers respond according to the film's interpretation of the situation. This interpretation is manifest in the film's formal features; in the way that the film works according to the stylistic choices of its makers.

If we all have the same interpretation of the arguing couple, as a result of the way that our attention has been focused on certain aspects of the narrative, Carroll claims it is not surprising that we all tend to respond in the way that the film intends. Thus the consistency puzzle is solved. While this account is highly appealing, it seems to contain a lacuna. This is because no explanation is given of why it is that, just because emotions provide focus, when this role is taken over by a film, the focus provided causes an emotion. An emotion's cause and its function are not one and the same, after all. But perhaps Carroll is simply relying on the fact that they are closely linked. The reason that emotions function as they do is in part because of the standard way that they come about. Thus, my anger is triggered by a perceived slight, but once it has been triggered, my anger serves to focus my attention on features of my situation which are relevant to having been slighted. If we are already focused on features of a film scene that are relevant to the standard trigger for a certain emotion, perhaps that emotion naturally tends to follow. Once completed, this kind of explanation could, in turn, complete Carroll's account.

Another version of this solution to the consistency puzzle focuses, not on the function of episodic, object-oriented emotional responses, but on the function of moods that pervade a film or significant portions of a film. Greg Smith argues that it is only by creating a mood that a film can maintain a consistent emotional appeal and reliably evoke the same emotional responses towards characters and events from different viewers.[203] Mood, on Smith's account, is a long-lasting and low-level feeling-state orienting us towards stimuli for particular emotional responses that in turn sustain the mood. If I am in a fearful mood as I walk home on a dark night, I am likely to notice frightening aspects of my environment – say, looming shadows and mysterious noises. In this way, the orientation of my mood makes me prone to respond with fear to a certain object, which in turn feeds back into my fearful mood and sustains it well past the subsidence of my particular fearful response. When I am in a fearful mood, I am not afraid of anything in particular from which I am motivated to flee or hide. But once I am interpreting my environment fearfully, I am more likely to have goal- and object-oriented responses of fear.

Even if, as Smith implies, every emotionally appealing film must sustain a mood, different films or film genres can accomplish this in more or less nuanced ways. Most action-adventure films, for example, do not aim at emotional subtlety. The mood of a typical film in this genre tends to be overshadowed by dense, often redundant, and highly foregrounded triggers or 'cues' for brief and focused emotional responses. At strategic moments in the film, there will be a cluster of emotional cues for, say, excitement and suspense – cues such as musical 'stingers' (sudden bursts of loud music), rapid cross-cutting or tracking shots, expressive close-up shots, an increase in the intensity or contrast of light, and an increase in the pace of action or the animation of the characters. The moments at which these cue-clusters occur tend to be strategic for narrative reasons. Indeed, one way in which emotional cues can be foregrounded is by tying them to narrative and character development. Thus if we are anxious to see the action hero escape from some deathly predicament, our emotional involvement in the moment can be heightened by the use of particular stylistic devices.

With his 'mood-cue approach' to solving the consistency puzzle, Smith also provides an explanation of how we come to share the overall feel of a film. Perhaps we are 'stirred up' by an action-adventure film such that we leave the cinema in an excitable mood. On Smith's account, this is likely to be the result of our having been cued at strategic points in the film to have particular emotional responses, which feed back into and sustain a particular mood. However, this leaves unanswered the question of how we catch the mood of a film in the first place for it then to be sustained by particular emotional responses. More importantly, it also leaves unanswered the question of why it is that subtle films with sparser and less foregrounded emotional cues – for example, *Tokyo Story* (1953) – are often the ones most likely to leave us in a certain mood. Part of an explanation could be that when we are not being bombarded by densely foregrounded emotional cues, we are better able to appreciate the mood behind the cues. But this does not explain why noticing the mood of a film makes it more likely for us to take up that mood.

Perhaps the mechanism involved is similar to the one involved in aspectual identification with characters: Insofar as the mood of a film is partly a matter of an attitude or point of view expressed in the overall look (and sound) of the film, we can take up this attitude in imagination and thus come to share the feeling that it involves. On the other hand, perhaps the mechanism involved is more visceral and automatic, involving less cognitive processing than identification. We will not decide this issue here, but it is certainly worth further thought and discussion as to how films not only stir us up in the moment but also have more lasting emotional effects.

CONCLUSIONS

This brings us to the end of our critical survey of philosophical issues to do with film and feeling. Here is what we have covered along the way:

1. A sketch of the traditional philosophical debate about the nature of emotions, and the recent move to more unified study of the full range of felt responses.
2. Solutions to the paradox of fiction, or how we can respond with genuine emotion to what we know is not real.
3. Solutions to the paradox of horror, or how we can enjoy the un-enjoyable emotions of fear and disgust in the context of horror fiction.
4. An acknowledgment of the fact that, despite theoretical suspicion of the notion, identification comes up regularly in ordinary discussions about the films we watch.
5. Metz's psychoanalytic account of primary identification with the camera which fails to capture the notion of identification invoked in ordinary discussions.
6. An alternative account of identification as a particular kind of imaginative activity which may also provide a unique form of insight into our own and others' responses.
7. The possibility of empathy, and not just sympathy, with film characters through imaginative identification.
8. The implications of our responsiveness to film form for the consistency of our responses to content.

We were able to proceed with our survey of film and feeling once we had determined that a solution to the paradox of fiction will likely follow from a deeper understanding of the nature of emotion. A solution to the paradox of horror also seems to depend on such an understanding, and in particular, on an understanding of what makes negative emotions negative such that they can still be enjoyed. There may be less reason, however, for thinking that the paradox of horror is really a paradox, given that it is unclear even for the greatest horror buff what he is really enjoying. Since horror films seem to be a case where our emotional responses duplicate the characters', this led us into a discussion of identification and empathy. We saw how the psychoanalytic notion of identification is distinct from the commonsense notion, but that if we account for identification as an imaginative activity, the possibility of duplicating a character's emotion becomes intelligible. Finally, by moving beyond the emotional appeal of characters, we discovered that this appeal is best explained in terms of the overall emotive structure of a film.

Perhaps this brings us as far as we can go with general theory, and what remains is close analysis of the effects of particular films. Such an analysis would surely give us an even greater appreciation of the extent to which film media are media of feeling.

NOTES

CHAPTER 1: FILM AS AN ART

1 These principles reflect the general anti-mimetic view that came to dominate the art world after the advent of non-objective painting. At that time, many critics and artists saw photography and film as liberating painting from the task of imitation. By completing this task mechanically, however, film and photography take the artistry out of the traditional aims of art.
2 Scruton (1995).
3 Ibid., 89.
4 King (1995).
5 This point is developed by Gaut (2002) in an extremely useful critique of Scruton.
6 King (1995: 118–20).
7 Arnheim (1957: 12).
8 Ibid., 26.
9 Ibid., 14.
10 Ibid., 16–17.
11 Ibid., 27–28
12 See Carroll (1988a: 58–70) for an assessment of Arnheim's ideas about art and expression.
13 Arnheim (1957: 35).
14 Ibid., 58.
15 For more examples of this kind, see Ibid., 60–64.
16 Arnheim's general point about the expressive use of the frame is illustrated in this way by Carroll in his (1988a: 41–42).
17 Arnheim's contemporaries, the Soviet-montage theorists, were particularly interested in the way that editing, or montage, can create artistic meaning and expression. For more on this, see Chapter 4.
18 Again, see Carroll (1988a: 58–75) for a critique of Arnheim's views on expression.
19 Arnheim (1957: 106).
20 See Sesonske (1973), (1974), and (1980).
21 Sesonske (1974: 52–53).
22 Ibid., 54.

23 Talk of a film 'representing space and time' is really just shorthand for saying that a film represents the spatial and temporal relations between objects and events. As well, talk of motion in film may or may not be literal, since there is an ongoing debate about whether the motion we see on screen is real or illusory. To learn about this debate, see Chapter 2.

24 Sesonske (1974: 54).

25 Ibid., 54–56.

26 Ibid., 56–57.

27 Ibid., 57.

28 This point is also made by Carroll in his (1988a: 31–32).

CHAPTER 2: REALISM

29 For example, Carroll, in his (1988a: 94), assigns singular importance to Bazin. Andrew Sarris, whose version of *auteur* theory we will consider in Chapter 3, also described Bazin as 'the greatest film critic who ever lived'.

30 Walton (1984).

31 Currie (1995a).

32 In his *Philosophy of Motion Pictures* (2008), Carroll gives a definition of film as an art form partly in terms of the technical possibility of the 'promotion of the impression of motion' (73).

33 Bazin (1967).

34 This useful summary list is provided by Carroll in his (1988a: 105–6).

35 Bazin (1967: 13–14).

36 Ibid., 14.

37 Ibid., 14–15.

38 Ibid., 15.

39 Ibid., 14.

40 In Carroll (1988a: 147–48).

41 Currie (1995a: 75–76).

42 Walton (1984: 250–51).

43 Bazin (1967: 14).

44 Walton (1984: 252).

45 Ibid., 261.

46 Currie (1995a: 55).

47 Walton (1984: 270).

48 Ibid., 270–71.

49 In particular, Currie (1995a) and Martin (1986).

50 Currie (1995a), chapter 3.

51 Friday (1996).

52 A theory according to which our everyday thought in some area has been tainted by a mistaken philosophical view such that it involves systematic errors.

53 The image that is made visible on a film screen or on photographic paper is a real image whereas an image in a (flat) mirror is a virtual image. In the photographic image, the rays of light are brought to a focus at the position of the image. The mirror-image, on the other hand, is made by rays of light that do not come from where the image seems to be. If I am standing two feet in front of a mirror, my image will appear 4 feet rather than 2 feet away from me – that is, 2 feet behind or inside the mirror.

54 Warburton (1988).

55 Walton (1997).

56 Friday (1996: 36).

57 Ibid., 39–40.

58 Many of the key features of Currie's account, including the notion of our 'recognitional capacities,' are drawn from the work of Flint Shier. See Shier (1986), particularly section 9.3.

59 Currie (1995a: 82–83).

60 Ibid., 83.

61 Ibid., 85.

62 Ibid., 100.

63 Ibid., 107.

64 This may be an over-simplified account of projection, since each image is often projected multiple times to reduce the flicker effect.

65 In what follows, I will refer to a particular article – Currie (1996) – which most fully presents Currie's account. Currie also discusses his account in the first chapter of his (1995a), and in the second section of his (1997).

66 Carroll (2008: 87–93).

67 In Adelson's checker shadow illusion, for example, we are shown an image of what appears to be a black and white checker-board with a green cylinder resting on it that casts a shadow diagonally across the middle of the board. The black and white squares are actually different shades of grey. The image has been constructed so that 'white' squares in the shadow, one of which is labelled 'B,' are actually the exact same grey value as 'black' squares outside the shadow, one of which is labelled 'A'. The illusion created is that the squares A and B are different colours (or shades).

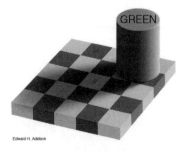

Edward H. Adelson

68 Currie (1996: 336).

69 Ibid., 248.

70 Kania (2002: 248).

71 Ibid., 249.

72 Ibid.

73 Ibid., 251.

74 Ibid.

75 Carroll (2008: 92).

76 Currie (1996: 326).

CHAPTER 3: AUTHORSHIP

77 Quoted by Stam (2000: 85).

78 Livingston (2005: 68–69). Practically the same definition is given by Livingston in an earlier essay, (1997).

79 Livingston (2005: 73).

80 Livingston (1997: 136).

81 Ibid., 135.

82 Livingston discusses in detail the conditions on joint authorship in his (2005: 75–89).

83 Livingston (1997: 135).

84 Nehamas (1986: 689).

85 Livingston (1997: 137). Given the variety of film-screening technologies, the current form of this definition may be too limited. Not all screened films are projected – films shown on television usually are not, for example. Nevertheless, there seems no reason why Livingston's definition could not be modified to accommodate technological variation.

86 Livingston (1997: 143–44).

87 Livingston (2005: 88).

88 Gaut (1997: 157).

89 Gaut (1997: 157–58).

90 Wollen (1972a).

91 Ibid., 171–72.

92 Livingston (1997: 145–46).

93 Sarris (1962/63: 105).

94 Ibid., 107.

95 Kael (1965).

96 Ibid., 298.

97 Ibid., 304.

CHAPTER 4: THE LANGUAGE OF FILM

98 As with the following examples: Spottiswoode (1950); and, Arijon (1976).
99 As with the following examples: Monaco (2000); and, McDonald (2005).
100 Goodman (1976).
101 Metz (1974b: 92).
102 Ibid., 107.
103 Currie (1995a: 117–18).
104 Pudovkin (1958: 121).
105 Ibid., 24.
106 Metz (1974a: 67).
107 Metz (1974c: 115).
108 Eisenstein (1957: 29–30).
109 Metz (1974a: 46).
110 Guzzetti (1985: 177–93).
111 Semiotic theorists can be called semiologists, semioticists, or semioticians. Given that 'semiologist' is often reserved for theorists working strictly in the tradition of Saussure, and given that 'semioticist' is the least common of the three terms, I prefer 'semiotician'.
112 Harman (1999: 92–93).
113 Wollen (1972b: 155).
114 Quoted by Harman in his (1999: 95).
115 Ibid., 96.
116 Currie (1995a: 121–22).
117 See, for example, Eco (1985).
118 The comparison between sentential connectives and shot/reverse-shot editing is made by Currie in his (2006: 97–98).
119 Currie (1995a: 135–36).

CHAPTER 5: NARRATION IN THE FICTION FILM

120 For a useful overview of the nature and value of narrative, see Livingston (2001).
121 Arguably, stories are not so much told in theatre performance as enacted. The fact remains, however, that narrative communication in theatre, as in film, is both visual and verbal.
122 See Kawin (1978).
123 See Wilson (1997a: 295–318).
124 Ibid., 310–11.
125 See Chatman (1990).

126 See Gaut (2004). It is also called the analytical argument by Kania in his (2005).

127 A version of this argument is put forward by Levinson in his (1996).

128 In fact, it is not clear that the narrator is always on the same ontological level as the fictional characters and events. An omniscient narrator may be considered to be 'outside' the story she is narrating even though she is still considered to be a fictional agent, part of the work of fiction.

129 These objections to the argument from means of access are made by Kania in his (2005).

130 See Wilson (1997a: 298–300).

131 Wolterstorff (1980: 172).

132 For seminal work in the debate about fiction, see Lewis (1978) and Searle (1979).

133 Currie (1995b).

134 Bordwell (1985: 62).

135 For a detailed introduction to the history and views of the group, see Erlich (1981).

136 Bordwell (1985: 49–51).

137 Ibid., 33–47.

CHAPTER 6: THE THINKING VIEWER

138 Bordwell (1985).

139 Bordwell (1989: 8).

140 Ibid., 8–9.

141 Wilson (1997b).

142 Bordwell (1985: 31).

143 Ibid., 32.

144 Ibid., 102.

145 This is suggested by Gaut in his (1995).

146 Bordwell (1989: 133).

147 Ibid., 3.

148 Bordwell and Thompson (1979: 119).

149 Gaut uses this example in his (1995: 18).

150 See Bordwell 2008.

151 The idea that the film viewer's search for narrative significance involves the framing and answering of questions is elaborated in a different context by Noël Carroll. According to Carroll, the basic structure of the most common form of film narrative is best conceived of as a network of questions and answers. Thus we can understand why a certain scene in a film follows another scene if we think of the earlier scene generating a question about

the narrative action that the later scene goes on to answer. For a detailed discussion of Carroll's 'erotetic' model of movie narration, see his (1988b) and his (2008).

152 Carroll first develops his theory of film evaluation in his (2003) and then refines his argument for the theory in chapter 7 of his (2008).

153 Carroll (2003: 147–48).

154 Here Carroll is drawing on Walton (1970) in which Walton argues that a work's aesthetic properties are to be found in a work when we perceive the work in the correct category. Carroll appropriates three of the four kinds of reasons that Walton gives for a correct categorization. The fourth kind of reason given by Walton that Carroll ignores has to do with a work providing the best kind of experience when perceived in a certain category.

155 Carroll (2003: 159–60).

156 See Freeland (2006) for some objections that Carroll does not anticipate in his earlier account of film evaluation, (2003), but which he then addresses in his most recent account, (2008: 213-17).

157 Carroll (2008: 213).

158 Ibid., 219.

159 Ibid., 220–21.

160 Ibid., 223.

161 Gaut (1995: 21–22).

162 Perkins (1993: 120).

163 Ibid., 131.

164 Ibid., 124–27.

165 Ibid., 190.

CHAPTER 7: THE FEELING FILM VIEWER

166 For a recent perceptual theory of emotion, see Prinz (2004). Roberts, in his (2003), characterizes emotions in terms of construal, which is analogous to the phenomenon of seeing-as. De Sousa, in his (1987), characterizes emotions as ways of seeing that precede the formation of beliefs and desires.

167 See, for example, Robinson (2005).

168 Alternatively, the paradox can be expressed, not in terms of how genuine emotions can be evoked by fiction, but in terms of whether responses to fiction really count as cases of genuine emotion. See Walton (1990: 197), Matravers (1998), and Neill (1995).

169 For example, Radford has a whole series of articles on the irrationality of our responses to fictions, beginning with his (1975).

170 The idea that we somehow suspend belief in the context of fiction can be attributed to Coleridge, although he talked about suspending disbelief,

meaning a belief in something that is not the case – that is, the reality of fiction. See his (1951). Carroll discusses the suspension of (dis)belief in his (1990).

171 See Walton (1990: 195–204, 241–55) for a famous version of this solution that appeals to the notion of make-believe.

172 See Lamarque (1981) as well as Carroll (1990: 79–88).

173 This and other objections are made by Walton in his (1990: 202–3).

174 See Carroll (1990) for a definition of the horror genre in terms of fear and disgust felt towards monsters.

175 This is the solution proposed by Carroll in his (1990: 158–95).

176 This expressivist solution is described though not endorsed by Gaut in his (1993).

177 Versions of the control solution are developed in Eaton (1982) and in Morreall (1985).

178 This example is adapted from Gaut (1993: 339).

179 See Gaut (1993).

180 See Carroll (2008) for an account of our engagement with film characters that takes a different focus. In chapter 6, Carroll argues that sympathy 'constitutes the major emotive cement between audiences and the pertinent movie characters' (178).

181 Mulvey (2000).

182 Metz's account of cinematic identification is developed in his (1982). For a helpful explication and critique of this account, see chapter 1 of Carroll (1988a).

183 Another reason to worry about the psychoanalytic account is that it implies that cinematic identification is pathological and thus undesirable or even dangerous. This implication springs from the fact that the viewer who identifies, according to Lacanian-inspired film theorists, is also a fetishist and a voyeur. According to Metz, the viewer fetishizes the material design of the film to compensate for the absence of what she is in fact most interested in; namely, what is shown on screen. Given this absence, there is no possibility of involvement with or detection by the film characters: The viewer becomes a passive and rather sneaky spectator – in other words, a voyeur.

184 Carroll (1990: 89).

185 See Wollheim (1984).

186 Ibid., 72.

187 See, for example, Carroll (1990: 88–96).

188 This kind of 'internal' understanding is discussed in Kieran (1996) and in Neill (1996).

189 Wollheim (1984: 79–80).

190 See Gaut (1999), particularly 206–16.

191 This point is made by Neill in his (1996).

192 These theorists include Feagin (1988) and Neill (1996).

193 Gaut (1999: 207).

194 Ibid., 211.

195 The same kind of response to Carroll is given by Gaut in his (1999: 207–8).

196 See Smith (1995: 98–101).

197 See Feagin (1988).

198 Both Neill, in his (1996), and Gaut, in his (1999), discuss the link between identification and understanding.

199 This example is adapted from Carroll (2008: 156–7).

200 See, once again, chapter 6 of Carroll (2008).

201 See, again, de Sousa (1987) and Roberts (2003).

202 This is a common view among psychologists and evolutionary biologists but it is also shared by Robinson (2005).

203 See Smith (1999) and (2003).

BIBLIOGRAPHY

Arijon, D. (1976), *Grammar of the Film Language* (London and Boston: Focal Press).

Arnheim, R. (1933), *Film*, tr. L. M. Sieveking and I. F. D. Morrow (London: Faber and Faber).

Arnheim, R. (1957), *Film as Art* (Berkeley: University of California Press).

Bazin, A. (1967), *What is Cinema?* ed. and tr. H. Grant (Berkeley and Los Angeles: University of California Press).

Bordwell, D. (2008), *Poetics of Cinema* (New York: Taylor and Francis).

Bordwell, D. (1985), *Narration in the Fiction Film* (Madison: University of Wisconsin Press).

Bordwell, D. (1989), *Making Meaning: Inference and Rhetoric in the Interpretation of Cinema* (Cambridge, MA: Harvard University Press).

Bordwell D. and Thompson, K. (1979), *Film Art: An Introduction* (New York: Alfred A. Knopf).

Carroll, N. (1988a), *Philosophical Problems of Classical Film Theory* (Princeton: Princeton University Press).

Carroll, N. (1988b), *Mystifying Movies: Fads and Fallacies in Contemporary Film Theory* (New York: Columbia University Press).

Carroll, N. (1990), *The Philosophy of Horror or Paradoxes of the Heart* (London and New York: Routledge).

Carroll, N. (2003), 'Introducing Film Evaluation', in *Engaging the Movie Image* (pp. 147–64) (New Haven and London: Yale University Press).

Carroll, N. (2008), *Philosophy of Motion Pictures* (Malden, MA: Blackwell).

Chatman, S. (1990), *Coming to Terms: The Rhetoric of Narrative in Fiction and Film* (Ithaca, NY: Cornell University Press).

Coleridge, S. T. (1951), *Biographia Literaria* in D. Stauffer (ed.), *Selected Poetry and Prose of Coleridge* (New York: The Modern Library, Random House).

Currie, G. (1995a), *Image and Mind: Film, Philosophy, and Cognitive Science* (New York: Cambridge University Press).

Currie, G. (1995b), 'Unreliability Refigured: Narrative in Literature and Film', *Journal of Aesthetics and Art Criticism* 53.1, 19–29.

Currie, G. (1996), 'Film, Reality, and Illusion', in D. Bordwell and N. Carroll (eds), *Post Theory: Reconstructing Film Studies* (pp. 325–44) (Madison: University of Wisconsin Press).

Currie, G. (1997), 'The Film Theory that Never Was: A Nervous Manifesto', in R. Allen and M. Smith (eds), *Film Theory and Philosophy* (pp. 42–59) (Oxford: Oxford University Press.

Currie, G. (2006), 'The Long Goodbye: The Imaginary Language of Film', in N. Carroll and J. Choi (eds), *Philosophy of Film and Motion Pictures: An Anthology* (pp. 91–99) (Malden, MA: Blackwell).

De Sousa, R. (1987), *The Rationality of Emotion* (Cambridge, MA: MIT Press).

Eaton, M. (1982), 'A Strange Kind of Sadness', *Journal of Aesthetics and Art Criticism* 41, 51–64.

Eco, U. (1985), 'On the Contribution of Film to Semiotics', in G. Mast and M. Cohen (eds), *Film Theory and Criticism: Introductory Readings*, Third edition (pp. 194–214) (New York and Oxford: Oxford University Press).

Eisenstein, S. (1957), 'The Cinematic Principle and the Ideogram', *Film Form and Film Sense*, ed. and tr. J. Leyda (pp. 28–44) (New York: Meridian).

Erlich, V. (1981), *Russian Formalism: History, Doctrine*, Third edition (New Haven: Yale University Press).

Feagin, S. (1988), 'Imagining Emotions and Appreciating Fiction', *Canadian Journal of Philosophy* 18.3, 485–500.

Freeland, C. (2006), 'Evaluating Film', *Film Studies* 8, 154–60.

Friday, J. (1996), 'Transparency and the Photographic Image', *British Journal of Aesthetics* 36.1, 30–42.

Gaut, B. (1993), 'The Paradox of Horror', *British Journal of Aesthetics* 33.4, 333–45.

Gaut, B. (1995), 'Making Sense of Films: Neoformalism and its Limits', *Forum for Modern Language Studies* XXXI.1, 8–23.

Gaut, B. (1997), 'Film Authorship and Collaboration', in R. Allen and M. Smith (eds), *Film Theory and Philosophy* (pp. 149–72) (Oxford and New York: Oxford University Press).

Gaut, B. (1999), 'Identification and Emotion in Narrative Film', in C. Plantinga and G. M. Smith (eds), *Passionate Views: Film, Cognition, and Emotion* (pp. 200–16) (Baltimore and London: Johns Hopkins University Press).

Gaut, B. (2002), 'Cinematic Art', *Journal of Aesthetics and Art Criticism* 60.4, 299–312.

Gaut, B. (2004), 'The Philosophy of the Movies: Cinematic Narration', in P. Kivy (ed.), *The Blackwell Guide to Aesthetics* (pp. 230–53) (Malden, MA: Blackwell).

Goodman, N. (1976), *Languages of Art* (Indianapolis: Hackett).

Guzzetti, A. (1985), 'Christian Metz and the Semiology of the Cinema', in G. Mast and M. Cohen, *Film Theory and Criticism: Introductory Readings*, Third edition (pp. 177–93) (New York and Oxford: Oxford University Press).

Harman, G. (1999), 'Semiotics and the Cinema: Metz and Wollen', in L. Braudy and M. Cohen (eds), *Film Theory and Criticism: Introductory Readings*, Fifth edition (pp. 90–8) (New York and Oxford: Oxford University Press).

Kael, P. (1965), 'Circles and Squares: Joys and Sarris', in *I Lost It at the Movies* (pp. 292–319) (Boston: Little, Brown, and Company).

Kania, A. (2002), 'The Illusion of Realism in Film', *British Journal of Aesthetics* 42.3, 243–58.

Kania, A. (2005), 'Against the Ubiquity of Fictional Narrators', *Journal of Aesthetics and Art Criticism* 63.1, 47–54.

Kawin, B. (1978), *Mindscreen: Bergman, Godard, and First-Person Film* (Princeton, NJ: Princeton University Press).

Kieran, M. (1996), 'Art, Imagination, and the Cultivation of Morals', *Journal of Aesthetics and Art Criticism* 54.4, 337–51.

King, W. (1995), 'Scruton and Reasons for Looking at Photographs', in A. Neill and A. Ridley (eds), *Arguing about Art: Contemporary Philosophical Debates* (pp. 114–21) (New York: McGraw-Hill).

Lamarque, P. (1981), 'How Can We Pity and Fear Fictions?' *British Journal of Aesthetics* 21.4, 291–304.

Levinson, J. (1996), 'Film Music and Narrative Agency', in D. Bordwell and N. Carroll (eds), *Post-Theory: Reconstructing Film Studies* (pp. 248–82) (Madison: University of Wisconsin Press).

Lewis, D. (1978), 'Truth in Fiction', *American Philosophical Quarterly* 15, 37–46.

Livingston, P. (1997), 'Cinematic Authorship', in R. Allen and M. Smith (eds), *Film Theory and Philosophy* (pp. 132–48) (Oxford and New York: Oxford University Press).

Livingston, P. (2001), 'Narrative', in B. Gaut and D. M. Lopes (eds), *The Routledge Companion to Aesthetics* (pp. 275–84) (London and New York: Routledge).

Livingston, P. (2005), *Art and Intention: A Philosophical Study* (Oxford, Clarendon Press).

Martin, E. (1986), 'On Seeing Walton's Great-Grandfather', *Critical Inquiry* 12, 796–800.

Matravers, D. (1998), *Art and Emotion* (Oxford: Clarendon Press).

McDonald, K. (2005), *Reading A Japanese Film: Cinema in Context* (Honolulu: University of Hawaii Press).

Metz, C. (1974a), 'The Cinema: Language or Language System?', in *Film Language: A Semiotics of the Cinema*, tr. M. Taylor (pp. 31–91) (New York: Oxford University Press).

Metz, C. (1974b), 'Some Points in the Semiotics of the Cinema,' *Film Language: A Semiotics of the Cinema*, tr. M. Taylor (pp. 92–107) (New York: Oxford University Press).

Metz, C. (1974c), 'Problems of Denotation in the Fiction Film', in *Film Language: A Semiotics of the Cinema*, tr. M. Taylor (pp. 108–46) (New York: Oxford University Press).

Metz, C. (1982), *The Imaginary Signifier: Psychoanalysis and the Cinema*, tr. C. Britton, A. Williams, B. Brewster, and A. Guzzetti (Bloomington: Indiana University Press).

Monaco, J. (2000), *How to Read A Film: The World of Movies, Media, Multimedia: Language, History, Theory*, Third edition (New York: Oxford University Press)

Morreall, J. (1985), 'Enjoying Negative Emotions in Fictions', *Philosophy and Literature* 19, 95–103.

Mulvey, L. (2000), 'Visual Pleasure and Narrative Cinema', in E. A. Kaplan (ed.), *Feminism and Film* (pp. 34–47) (Oxford University Press).

Nehamas, A. (1986), 'What an Author Is', *Journal of Philosophy* 83.11, 685–91.

Neill, A. (1995), 'Feelings and Fictions', in A. Neill and A. Ridley (eds), *Arguing about Art: Contemporary Philosophical Debates* (pp. 175–93) (New York: McGraw-Hill).

Neill, A. (1996), 'Empathy and (Film) Fiction', in D. Bordwell and N. Carroll (eds), *Post-Theory: Reconstructing Film Studies* (pp. 175–94) (University of Wisconsin Press).

Perkins, V. F. (1993), *Film as Film: Understanding and Judging Movies* (New York: De Capo Press).

Prinz, J. (2004), *Gut Reactions: A Perceptual Theory of Emotion* (New York: Oxford University Press).

Pudovkin, V. I. (1958), *Film Technique and Film Acting*, tr. and ed. I. Montagu (New York, Grover Press).

Radford, C. (1975), 'How Can We Be Moved by the Fate of Anna Karenina? Part 1', *Aristotelian Society: Supplementary Volume* 49, 67–80.

Roberts, R. C. (2003), *Emotions: An Essay in Aid of Moral Psychology* (Cambridge and New York: Cambridge University Press).

Robinson, R. (2005), *Deeper than Reason: Emotion and its Role in Literature, Music, and Art* (Oxford: Clarendon Press).

Sarris, A. (1962/63), Notes on the '*Auteur* Theory in 1962', *Film Culture* 27, 1–8.

Schier, F. (1986), *Deeper into Pictures: An Essay on Pictorial Representation* (Cambridge: Cambridge University Press).

Scruton, R. (1995), 'Photography and Representation', in A. Neill and A. Ridley (eds), *Arguing about Art: Contemporary Philosophical Debates* (pp. 89–113) (New York: McGraw-Hill).

Searle, J. (1979), 'The Logical Status of Fictional Discourse', in *Expression and Meaning: Studies in the Theory of Speech Acts* (pp. 58–75) (Cambridge: Cambridge University Press).

Sesonske, A. (1973), 'Cinema Space', in D. Carr and E. Casey (eds), *Explorations in Phenomenology* (pp. 399–409) (The Hague: Martinus Nijhoff).

Sesonske, A. (1974), 'Aesthetics of Film, or A Funny Thing Happened on the Way to the Movies', *Journal of Aesthetics and Art Criticism* 33.1, 51–7.

Sesonske, A. (1980), 'Time and Tense in Cinema', *Journal of Aesthetics and Art Criticism* 38.4, 419–26.

Smith, G. M. (1999), 'Local Emotions, Global Moods, and Film Structure', in C. Plantinga and G. M. Smith (eds), *Passionate Views: Film, Cognition, and Emotion* (pp. 103–26) (Baltimore: Johns Hopkins University Press).

Smith, G. M. (2003), *Film Structure and the Emotion System* (Cambridge and New York: Cambridge University Press).

Smith, M. (1995), *Engaging Characters: Fiction, Emotion, and the Cinema* (Oxford: Clarendon Press).

Spottiswoode, R. (1950), *A Grammar of the Film: An Analysis of Film Technique* (Berkeley: University of California Press).

Stam, R. (2000), *Film Theory: An Introduction* (Malden, MA: Blackwell).

Walton, K. (1970), 'Categories of Art', *Philosophical Review* 79, 334–67.

Walton, K. (1984), 'Transparent Pictures: On the Nature of Photographic Realism' *Critical Inquiry* 11, 246–77.

Walton, K. (1990), *Mimesis as Make-Believe: On the Foundations of the Representational Arts* (Cambridge, MA: Harvard University Press).

Walton, K. (1997), 'On Pictures and Photographs: Objections Answered', in R. Allen and M. Smith (eds), *Film Theory and Philosophy* (pp. 60–75) (Oxford: Clarendon Press).

Warburton, N. (1988), 'Seeing Through "Seeing Through" Photographs', *Ratio* 1, 62–74.

Wilson, G. (1997a), '*Le Grand Imagier* Steps Out: The Primitive Basis of Film Narration', *Philosophical Topics* 25, 295–318.

Wilson, G. (1997b), 'On Film Narrative and Narrative Meaning', in R. Allen and M. Smith (eds), *Film Theory and Philosophy* (pp. 221–38) (Oxford: Clarendon Press).

Wollen, P. (1972a), 'The *Auteur* Theory', in *Signs and Meaning in the Cinema* (pp. 74–115) (Bloomington: Indiana University Press).

Wollen, P. (1972b), 'The Semiology of the Cinema', in *Signs and Meaning in the Cinema* (pp. 116–55) (Bloomington: Indiana University Press).

Wollheim, R. (1984), *The Thread of Life* (Cambridge, MA: Harvard University Press).

Wolterstorff, N. (1980), *Works and Worlds of Art* (Oxford: Oxford University Press).

Index